Readers of *Cornucopia* are familiar with the writing of Azize Ethem from her Village Voices, her delightful diary of daily life in Iznik, where she and her husband Selim have built a home on the shores of Lake Ascania. Her earlier articles described life in their previous home in the village of Dereköy on the southern coast of Turkey, where they settled after first moving to Turkey from Saudi Arabia. Her new book, Beyond the Orchard, describes the trials and tribulations of building a house and starting a new life in a tiny Turkish village, she, an expatriate Englishwoman, and he, an Ottoman prince from the imperial Osmanlı dynasty who had been exiled when the Turkish Republic was founded in 1923.

In the prologue Azize describes a scene in Dereköy fourteen years later, in the shop of Hamza, the village tailor. A summer resident, a retired officer from Ankara, enters the shop and, after chiding Hamza for not having *finished* a repair to his waistcoat, addresses Azize, who is sitting there silently sipping tea with the village elders.

Turning to me, the man asked me curtly in German where I was from. 'From the Village,' I replied. 'Rubbish,' he said as he turned to Hamza and asked where I was from. Without looking up from his work, our tailor said, 'She's from the Village.' Barking his question to each of the ancients in turn, he asked where I was from and each replied that I was from Dereköy. He made a sort of humphing snorting sound and marched out of the shop. We sat in silence again until I asked where the gentleman was from. One of the men looked up and, with a dismissive wave of his hand, said, 'Ankara...He's a foreigner.' Fourteen years had passed since I, the first foreigner to live in Dereköy, had arrived. I had, hopefully, learned the ways of my neighbours and they, in turn, tolerated mine. By now I am one of them, a villager. To me there is no greater accolade.

Such is the spirit of *Beyond the Orchard*, a beautifully written, witty and evocative book that should be read by all foreigners living in Turkey as well as by the Turks with whom they dwell, for this is a classic that tells of how people get on with one another at the village level in Anatolia, where communal living began ten thousand years ago.

John Freely

© Çitlembik / Nettleberry Publications, 2004
All Rights Reserved

Editor: Carol LaMotte
Drawings: Trici Venola

ISBN: 975-6663-69-3

In Turkey:
Şeyh Bender Sokak 18/1
Asmalımescit - Tünel
80050 Istanbul
www.citlembik.com.tr

In the USA:
Nettleberry LLC
44030 123rd St.
Eden, South Dakota 57232
www.nettleberry.com

Printed at Berdan Matbaası:
Davutpaşa Cad. Güven San. Sit.
C-Blok No: 215-216 Topkapı Istanbul, Turkey
Tel: (0212) 613 12 11 - 613 11 12

BEYOND THE ORCHARD

Azize Ethem

Çitlembik Publications 70

ACKNOWLEDGEMENTS

I wish to thank Berrin Torolsan Scott, Editor of Cornucopia, for her encouragement over the years, and for permitting me to use material previously published in Cornucopia.

Azize Ethem

To Sara, Julian and Selim
(in the order of their appearance in my life), with love.

PROLOGUE

I WAS SITTING on a large brown paper parcel in the village tailor's cramped little shop waiting for a pair of my husband's trousers to be altered, three of the village patriarchs watching as Hamza threaded his antiquated but rather complicated machine. We sat in companionable silence sipping our glasses of tea, brought from the tea-house across the road. Two tourists in the shortest of shorts stood in the sun waiting for what they thought was the hourly bus, already running late. Osman the driver ignored them as he continued to play tavla under the huge mulberry tree. Hussein the postman called out something rude to Songül the grocer's wife as she laughed and shook her fist at him. Inside the dark shop dust softened the rays of sunlight and the air was heavy with tobacco smoke and the smell of well-worn clothes.

We all looked up when there was a hearty greeting from

the door, and a very dapper elderly gentleman strode into the shop. It was very difficult to actually stride, with most of the floor space occupied by the audience sitting on stools as well as the large parcel and me. From the quality of his tweed jacket and the man's manner it was easy to see that he was a city man, one of the summer people who arrive from Istanbul or Ankara each year. I tabbed him as 'retired military' and this was reinforced by his authoritative tone as he began to chide Hamza for not having finished a repair to his waistcoat. Hamza shrugged his shoulders and didn't appear to be the slightest bit concerned by the lecture.

Turning to me, the man asked me curtly in German where I was from. "From the Village," I replied in Turkish. "Rubbish," he said as he turned to Hamza and asked where I was from. Without looking up from his work, our tailor said, "She's from the Village." Barking his question to each of the ancients in turn, he asked where I was from and each replied that I was from Dereköy. He made a sort of humphing snorting sound and marched out of the shop.

We sat in silence again until I asked where the gentleman was from. One of the men looked up and, with a dismissive wave of his hand, said, "Ankara...He's a foreigner."

Fourteen years had passed since I, the first foreigner to live in Dereköy, had arrived. I had, hopefully, learned the ways of my neighbours and they, in turn, tolerated mine. But now I am one of them, a villager. To me there is no greater accolade.

CHAPTER 1.

MY NEW LIFE in a Turkish village was prompted by a conversation one evening as we were driving home along the
Corniche in Jeddah, after yet another farewell party. Dot
and Jim were off to a bungalow in Brighton, she with her
Bedouin jewellery and he with a collection of Saudi stories,
off to bore and be bored. We had seen so many friends
leave with high hopes only to realize that life after retire-
ment was not all it was cracked up to be. Several of Selim's
colleagues, after years of saving for a comfortable old age,
had dropped dead within months of moving into their
dream homes.

When Selim gloomily remarked that it would be our
turn in ten years, I broached the subject of a suicide pact.
After a long silence he said, "We could retire tomorrow if
we settled in Turkey." "Fine," I said. "Let's go." I don't
remember any further discussion, no sensible examination

of the pros and cons, although we did get the OK from the children when they arrived home from England for the school holidays. For Selim it was a return to his roots; for me a new adventure beckoned.

After twenty years in Saudi Arabia, my husband dreamed of water and lush vegetation. Within weeks we were off to find our dream plot of land; the requirements were simple: a small village near the sea. All very straightforward, we thought. Marmaris had been perfect when Selim visited the town ten years earlier.

The first time my husband had brought us to Turkey we were prepared to see an Islamic nation more lenient than Saudi...just how lenient was a very pleasant surprise. On arriving at the airport, the first thing we saw was a flock of nuns. Saus commented that perhaps it was a Turkish national costume. Coming from a country where bibles are forbidden, we couldn't believe they were really nuns. Within minutes we saw a Jewish rabbi, and our confusion was complete. Selim gave us yet again his lecture on Turkey being a secular state, tolerant of non-Islamic faiths; this time we believed him.

That first day, after settling into a small hotel in Bebek on the shores of the Bosphorus, we went out to explore. Selim, so proud of his homeland, guided us through narrow streets as he pointed out various shops. Pog gave me a sharp nudge as we were being regaled with the details of the different breads and Turkish sweets. Following my son's gaze, I was horrified to see that the shelves of bread were covered with mouse droppings, with drifts piled in the corners of the shelves. It took a week for our patriotic guide to notice the three of us were not eating bread; when at breakfast he queried our new diet, Saus hesitantly pointed to a mouse dropping on the basket of bread. To our embarrassment, we were told about the seed of a plant called "Love-in-a-Mist".

On closer inspection it was a little smaller than the visiting card of a mouse, and we learned another lesson about judging a culture through ignorant eyes.

My most vivid memory of that first visit was when Saus and I had ventured out alone. It was at a time when there was a larger military presence in the city than usual and soldiers on street corners were a common sight. We were walking past the entrance to Gülhane Park near Topkapi Palace where a group of conscripts were digging a flowerbed while a sergeant oversaw their work. As we drew closer to the group, there was a sharp command and the young men quickly formed a line. As we drew level, at another command from the sergeant they presented arms, handling their weapons with a smooth synchronised action. As a soldier's daughter, I was impressed by the precision and discipline of the manoeuvre and filled with joy. I am sure few young girls, with mother in tow, have been honoured by a platoon of young Turkish squaddies armed with shovels.

Sometimes we would visit Istanbul without burdening relatives with our presence, and like two children playing truant, we would explore the city. I think one could explore Istanbul for a year and still not see every interesting corner.

On this occasion there would be no avoiding the round of family visits. Even before our taxi pulled up outside the family house on the Asian shore I was clammy with the thought of the ordeal ahead. Why I allowed myself to be intimidated by "The Aunt", I have never understood. Brought up as a princess of the Ottoman Dynasty, she had lived a long and gracious life. Gentle and sweet, she had always had her own way until I came bumbling into her life. I was not what she had planned for her beloved nephew and in the nicest possible way I was repeatedly made aware of exactly how she felt. A French- woman may have been passable at a push, but an Englishwoman past her prime with two children was totally unacceptable.

The wizened gnome who answered the door had been a family retainer for decades; age had chipped away his responsibilities, but opening the door to guests of rank was a duty he tenaciously clung to. Tears of joy ran down his cheeks and, having executed his best Uriah Heep salaam to Selim, he allowed himself to be assisted back to his little stool by the salon door. From this perch he would monitor every conversation while keeping a rheumy eye on the maid and cleaning woman. As Selim moved to kiss the royal hand, a cheek was turned for him. I was permitted to act out the full hand- kissing grovel without the honour of a cheek being offered. The maid guided me to a plush velvet sofa a little removed from centre stage. Sitting very primly, it was only seconds before I realised the sofa had very recently been cleaned and the damp was fast seeping into my skirt. The Olympic athlete's deodorant with a dryness guarantee was fast failing as I wilted under the watchful eyes of the imperial ancestors glowering from their ornate frames. My one slight wriggle of discomfort was all our gracious hostess needed, and expressing her sorrow that I didn't speak French or Turkish, she suggested I might like to explore the garden. Outside, heady with the sense of freedom, I sat on the patio under the overgrown grapevines. The wraith-like cleaning woman silently appearing with tea and cakes gently patted my cheek, and standing me up, slipped my skirt round so the sun could dry the damp patches.

Before heading south to our idyllic hamlet, we ran the usual gauntlet of the round of family visits. While all have heard of the Chinese water torture, little is known of the Ottoman tea torture. At every turn we were plied with tea and cakes, glass after glass, plate after plate of cakes, with never a soul having to head for the bathroom. Heaped with cakes the consistency of very dry shortbread, a plate was handed to each guest, accompanied by a small glass of strong black tea. Battling my way through the plateful with my palate clogged with a biscuity paste, I would need my tea-glass constantly refilled. Brought up to eat everything on my plate, once having emptied it, I would find it whisked away and replenished. More shortbread equalled more tea. More tea equalled a visit to the lavatory. The Aunt would smile sweetly as I grew more uncomfortable and was forced to ask for the bathroom. I could almost hear them adding the crime of being weak-bladdered to my list of shortcomings. On the third day of our refreshment trek I secreted a plastic bag in my handbag, and with a Houdini sleight of hand managed to off-load platefuls. This dexterity cut down on tea consumption and bathroom visits, with every hostess glowing with satisfaction as I cleaned my plate.

While all approved of the wanderer's return, the idea of living anywhere but the city was unthinkable. To settle in a village was obviously the foolish idea of a foreign wife. Eventually we were free and heading south. Fortunately for Marmaris (perhaps) but not for us, the fertile fields of this sleepy town had blossomed with dense rows of hotels and discos. Ghettos of holiday houses in white clumps perched on the surrounding hills along with all the wonders that go hand in hand with tourism. Young men adorned the shop doorways looking nothing like the young Turks of our memories. Thumbs hooked in the pockets of tight jeans with hips thrust forward, they looked as if they were advertising codpieces rather than carpets, leather jackets or kebab houses. After our initial shock and a night in a hotel with an English pub theme, we visited a real estate agent who promised to guide us further afield to our special village with that perfect piece of land.

For two weeks we travelled tortuous roads to view barren acres with huge electricity pylons, places where you could get a glimpse of the sea if you built a four-story home, land abutting highways, acres where every tree had been felled. We saw the lot. Dispirited but hopeful, I stayed on while Selim went back to Saudi; I continued the almost-daily trips to inspect totally unsuitable land. By the time Selim returned a few weeks later, I'd met every real estate agent and seen all on the books.

In spite of my lack of success, my beloved was rather chirpy and announced that The Aunt had friends who lived in a village named Dereköy; he was taking me to lodge with these people. I'd be safe there while I looked for land. He had to return to Jeddah in a week, and the thought of me being with friends calmed his eastern sense of propriety.

I sulked as we drove over beautiful hills, and when he tried to break the ice by pointing out the flowering oleander bushes, I tersely said, "They're poisonous." I was ungrateful; the friends were sweet and welcoming. Selim arranged to pay for my lodgings and we started to look for land.

The village of less than one hundred houses was situated at the foot of a rugged mountain at the end of a 60-mile turquoise bay on the Aegean Sea. The villagers were market gardeners, fishermen or employees of the Forestry Department. There were a few citrus orchards and olive groves between the fields of vegetables and sesame. The mountains on each side of the bay were pine-clad and only a mile inland a river emerged from nowhere, fed by underground lakes. Although there were a handful of summer homes, it was not a fashionable spot like Marmaris or Bodrum. The soil was rich and the fishing good, nobody had to work too hard to make ends meet, and nobody wanted more than that. The heart of the village had grown up around the intersection of the old pre-Roman road that skirted the foot of the mountains and the new road which leads to the highway. The bakery with its huge pile of firewood sat next to the village headman's office on one corner of the crossroads. There was a pair of barber's shops, two grocery stores selling identical goods, a butcher's, and a haberdashery with a few faded ribbons and a lot of dead flies in the window. The tailor's shop with its rusting corrugated iron awning, along with the fishing tackle and gas-bottle store, perched below the mosque. The ramshackle teahouse with mismatched tables and chairs arranged under a massive mulberry tree took up one complete corner, with the post and telegraph office opposite. Fish could be purchased down at the pier when the boats returned with their catch, and for anything else one had to travel 25 miles over the mountains to Muğla. Down by the shore, several restaurants competed for business, all sporting the same menu. As I wandered inland along the old road, I would meet the shepherdess with her small flock; she would be talking to her charges in her thin sing-song voice as she spun wool on a wooden spindle. Ancient and nimble, she would present me with a sprig of wild marjoram or thyme, never questioning my presence or stopping to talk. Just a mile along the low road were three Carian tombs. One of them had the ornate temple façade common to the region, but the other two were unadorned, with simple square entrances cut into the rock. When I was told that they would have had large stones rolled in front of the door, I wondered if they were the same as the tomb Joseph of Arimathea had built in Jerusalem. Sitting by the tombs, surrounded by the perfume of wild herbs, it was as if time had stood still.

A beautiful village, yes, but our piece of land, no. Selim returned to Jeddah and, alone again, I viewed another batch of sites, the friends baffled by my lack of ability to see the benefits of a house on the edge of the main road or a flat above the bakery.

Back in Dereköy, Selim returned from the teahouse one morning with Ahmet the taxi driver. Why, Selim asked our host, had he not told us about the land Ahmet had found? It's half a mile from the village and not what you want, was the reply. Selim, in his most WOG (Worthy Oriental Gentleman) manner, said that we would look at it all the same.

We drove down a winding track bordered by overgrown

hedgerows on each side, stopping in front of a high wall with pieces of ancient capitals and columns cemented between the rough-hewn stones. The owner, a huge elderly man, welcomed us at the gate and led us through his mandarin and orange grove to the end of the land, where the 3000 square metres he wished to sell ran in a ribbon along the edge of the river. Here, at the end of his property, he had planted eucalyptus trees ten years earlier and the heady scent of the gum leaves filled the air. As I stood in the grove intersected by streams running to the river, I couldn't look at Selim. There were the towering mountains behind the village, and to the east, beyond the river and marshland, another line of mountains and foothills. Kingfishers zipped between the reeds; herons and egrets strutted on the marsh while a golden eagle soared high above the bay. The river was deep and clean, with not a building as far as the eye could see. The only sounds were those of the rustling branches, the birdsong and the splashing brooks. It was heaven, perfect, and if Selim didn't like it I would die. He seemed disinterested but said he'd meet Baba Macit, the owner, that evening in the tea house.

Back in the taxi he asked Ahmet to drop us at the beach cafe and when we were finally alone he asked what I thought of it. "It's wonderful," I answered as he grinned. "Great! I was worried you wouldn't like it," he said. I was forbidden to look happy, to even think of sneaking back to have another look; any flicker of interest would raise the price. In the teahouse that evening, a figure was agreed upon and hands were shaken. That was that: a handshake to Baba Macit was as good as a legal document.

Our host could not believe we had done something so utterly stupid. "A very bad buy," was his verdict - no village water supply, no road and too far out of the village. "Poor soil," said the villagers. "It floods in winter and the mosquitoes will eat you." We didn't care; it was our very own little slice of paradise.

Now that it was settled, as we picnicked under the trees, we spent hours planning where to build the house. Selim hired a dilapidated fishing boat and we explored the river to its mouth, less than a mile from its source. We would motor upstream and float silently back down. One evening just before dusk we saw an otter playing with her three kits: tumbling in the water they looked like sleek wet kittens. As we floated by, the mother watched us closely but made no move to leave or interrupt the game.

Selim arranged for a lawyer his family knew to come from Istanbul and conduct the land transaction, and off he went to Saudi to pack our belongings and return in a month for good.

The great day dawned, with the lawyer arriving and us joining a modest convoy of vehicles to drive the 10 miles over the mountains to the town where the title deed office was located. Baba Macit was accompanied by two aged cronies, and driven by his grandson. Two well-built head-scarved matrons being chauffeured in a battered van turned out to be Baba's daughters. Mesut the lawyer and I travelled with Ahmet in the old Opel taxi.

On arrival, we caused an interesting diversion for the teahouse patrons; all knew Baba Macit and the accompanying villagers. Everyone had to be brought up to date on Dereköy events, and six of them joined our group to assist with advice and banter.

Mesut Bey commandeered a poor intimidated little civil servant's office and proceeded to slowly type a long document, which he bullied Baba and his daughters to sign. Only at this stage did I realise that none of the three was able to read, though they could painstakingly sign their names. Weeks later, I learned that the document demanded full refund of our money if for any reason we could not build our planned home.

By this stage I had taken a strong dislike to the family

lawyer, so obsequious to me, but treating my new friends as if they were a sub-species far down the primate scale.

To ease the legalities, the land was being bought in The Aunt's name, and Mesut Bey flourished an impressive power of attorney while he browbeat and hurried those who had to sign what to me were mysterious sheaves of paper. Stamps were licked and affixed, rubber stamps were wielded, and in ten minutes the official transaction was done.

Hands were shaken all round and, as everyone thanked everyone else, it was obviously time for tea and a gossip. Gülşen, one of the stout daughters, was having trouble with her ankles and was ensconced on a dusty bench, discussing parsley with a newcomer. I felt very much part of it all, having recognised one word in her sentence, but a little deflated that what was being said about parsley was beyond my linguistic skills. Gülşen was roused as my nasty legal man harried us, like a well-trained dog moving a flock of sheep. Keeping us in a neat group with no stragglers, he herded us off to the bank.

The bank manager and staff awaited us in a line at the door to shake hands; while I was salaamed into the manager's office, Mesut Bey was given a slightly less impressive chair than mine. Baba Macit and the gaggle of villagers were left to stand at the office door. There was a moment of consternation when I insisted that seats be found for Baba and his daughters. My triumph over this blow for equality was dampened by the obvious discomfort of the newly seated three.

The bank staff had prepared an account for Baba; dollars were deleted from my account and liras put into his. The new bankbook was presented with a flourish, but Baba was no fool. He had been promised a sum of money, not a useless book; he'd had enough of the Istanbul outsider as well as the bank manager. His wrath was most impressive – the bank was going to lose a new account and suddenly Baba was a VIP. After much discussion, he was taken to the bank safe and shown his money, which would be kept for him in safety. He could come and look at it any time and could take it whenever he wanted. He turned his back on the hierarchy and, after a long discussion with the bank "tea boy," who was, I gather, the 60-year-old nephew of a friend, he decided this was a sensible system. He accepted the little book with the air of an international businessman, and that was the cue for us all to repeat the handshaking ritual.

Mesut Bey gave our driver a curt nod and hustled me to the Opel to set off back across the mountains. Leaning from the front seat, the family's man from Istanbul told me in hesitant French that it was wise not to get involved with the locals. Although with my scant knowledge of the language I got the gist of it, I pretended not to understand him and told him to...well...I used a deliciously vulgar Arabic phrase. He didn't understand the words but he certainly sensed the tone, and the stony silence lasted until we reached the village.

Ahmet was to drive him to the airport to catch the evening flight back to civilisation. Leaving me in the village, he went to shake my hand but I quickly turned my palm down and he was forced to kiss my hand, then place it to his forehead. I might be new around here, but I'd learned the rules from a master.

Next day I found I'd been left the taxi bill.

CHAPTER 2.

FINALISING THINGS IN Jeddah was not going to be as swift as we had thought; Selim was going to be a long time, probably months before he could get to Dereköy permanently. I had to find somewhere to live until we had a house on the land. My landlord and his wife were so caring, kind and helpful, I felt stifled. If I sat under a tree to read, one of them would join me; if I went for a walk I would be accompanied by them or their daughter. Escaping to my room, there would be a knock on the door to ask if there was a problem. When I mentioned renting a little house, there were tears and they asked why I didn't like them. A few days later I met a delightful couple who spoke English; they told me they were neighbours of my guardians. I expressed surprise that we hadn't met, and when they looked uncomfortable I realised that I hadn't been introduced to anyone in the village. They were just inviting me to pop in any time for tea when my chaperone returned and hustled me out of the shop.

By the time Selim reappeared once again, I had made firm friends with Solmaz and her husband Aydın. These two wonderful people were to guide me through the intricacies of the Turkish social niceties and smooth my path over the ensuing years. With their help, Selim was convinced that I could survive without constant supervision, and a small village house was found for me to make a home. Somehow I was transferred from house-guest status to householder with no ill feelings or ruffled feathers. Perhaps my host and hostess were secretly pleased to see the back of such a graceless and difficult guest.

My landlady Şahide lived next door with her teenage son. Her constant companion was an ancient dog named Ateş, meaning fire. I presume the forestry guards knew her voice, as her habit of standing at the door and bellowing the word 'fire' never instigated the setting off of the village fire siren. Her husband had died in a gruesome accident and, as her boy had no inclination to work, her only income was from the occasional rental of the little house at the end of her land. Whitewashed inside and out, standing in the garden among the pomegranate trees, the house looked perfect; inside, it left a lot to be desired. The bathroom, a small windowless concrete bunker, had a tap with a piece of garden hose attached and a jagged hole in the corner to drain away water. The lavatory was the top half of a western pedestal balanced over a second hole in the concrete; a jug of water hurled from a great height was the only flushing mechanism. The kitchen had a wooden bench, one tap and a plastic bowl. Wastewater could be tossed out the window or poured down the hole in the corner of the bathroom. Two bedrooms came equipped with ancient iron bedsteads with damp, amazingly lumpy cotton-filled mattresses. The living room had a rickety table, a chair and a plastic stool. Selim was horrified, but I was ecstatic.

Armed with a long shopping list, with our new-found

friends we headed over the mountains to Muğla, the capital of the province. The men went off to buy mattresses, a refrigerator and kitchen stove while Solmaz led me to the Thursday market. There were acres of vegetables, pots and pans, with pyramids of eggs next to piles of twig brooms. Elastic belts for subduing hernias and leeches in bottles for medicinal use jostled for space beside bales of locally woven cotton fabrics. Weighed down with parcels, we made our way to a local café where the owner, a Dereköy resident, packed our purchases in his ancient van and, assuring us there was room for more, promised to deliver them on his way home that evening. Solmaz knew every corner of the market, and we bustled through the maze of narrow streets to the towel shop, another stall for sheets and yet another for pillowcases. Meeting up with Selim and Aydın, we were flushed with success as we crossed scores of items off the list.

In a flurry of domesticity I hand-sewed curtains, bed-spreads and large squishy cushions for seating in the living room. Selim levelled the table legs, made poles for the cur-tains and shelves for the kitchen. A huge plastic bowl in the bathroom doubled as a washing machine and bath, with the hot water having to be carried pan by pan from the kitchen stove.

At last settled, albeit less than comfortably, we turned our thoughts to building a house down by the river.

Selim asked the men at the teahouse who had built the five new-ish traditional houses in the village. These buildings stood out among the concrete boxes complete with metal window frames, which the locals considered modern and superior. We were told that a well known elderly local poet-cum-architect had started a campaign to revive interest in traditional building styles. A visit to this man and his wife filled me with excitement when I found that they understood exactly what we wanted. It was decided that we should build a small cottage to start with and later embark on the house of our dreams further along our land. Nail Bey drew a cottage and floor plan on a paper serviette as I gazed around their beautiful home, a replica of the very old house in a nearby village that Nail Bey had lived in as a child. I would have taken more interest if I had realised this was the completed plan, with no more cosy chats or dithering to be indulged in. The sketch on the flimsy paper was transformed into a formal plan by an architect in Muğla and for the princely sum of about £4 sterling the village head-man stamped it as having passed the scrutiny of the building committee. Selim talked money with the poet, and a date to start building was agreed on. The salon, which was an extremely grand name for our sitting area, was to be hexa-gonal, while the kitchen and our bedroom were to have a bay wall. (That is a bay window minus the window.) Through some oversight, or perhaps a crease in the serviette, the bathroom was to be square.

With Selim once more absent, Baba Macit ignored his mandarin grove and took on the role of foreman. He supervised the marking out of the foundations, done rather haphazardly with string and eucalyptus sticks. He shouted and waved his arms at the bulldozer driver who cleared a track from the road. The driver, who had borrowed the machine, turned out to be the owner of the lemon orchard next door, and as a welcome present he announced that all the lemons on the tree nearest my new path would in future be mine. A grandiose gesture, I thought, but each year the fruit-pickers left my tree heavy with fruit.

Piles of lumber, bricks, stone and sand were delivered, to be joined under the trees by roof tiles, bathroom fittings and even the kitchen sink. Soon it was time to start digging the foundations, and as Selim had insisted that no tree was to be cut down to allow machinery onto the site, the foun-dations were to be dug by hand. Every worker who had delivered materials, the Muğla architect, the poet and, of course, Baba knew with no room for doubt that the first shovel of earth removed would uncover a spring. As springs dotted the land, forming streams that meandered to the river, even I, a dedicated Pollyanna, was worried.

Arriving at 7 a.m. on 'Foundation Day,' I found Baba Macit already ensconced on an ancient kitchen chair he'd brought down from his house. He was well into Sergeant Major mode, bullying two placid, smiling workers. All three greeted me with the usual pleasantries and then assured me that we would need a pump by lunch time. The head digger was an elderly man named Nabi, with his son making up the excavation team. Nabi, who looked too worn and frail to do any work, lifted enormous rocks, which he then piled outside the growing hole. Rocks that looked too large for any man to lift were cradled in his arms as he staggered to the edge of the small crater.

Later in the morning, Baba sent me to the village to buy goats' cheese, strong brown onions, tomatoes and four loaves of bread for lunch. The men in the teahouse and the shopkeepers called, "*Pompa...Pompa*," nodding and smiling at me in their wisdom while I, the stupid foreign woman, feigned a nonchalant air. I had no idea where a pump would come from or how the promised gushing water would be re-routed, but there was no way I was going to let them see my concern. My only glimmer of hope was that our friend Aydın, as a mining engineer, would know all about flooded pits; hopefully he would know where to get the damned *pompa* as well.

I dallied as I returned with lunch; the hedgerows were full of wrens and robins. There were many birds I did not recognise and I vowed to get a book sent out from England. I met the goat-lady slowly making her way down the lane as her charges stood on their hind legs to nibble the new shoots in the hedgerow. The camel-man passed me with his two beasts loaded with firewood, his fat little dog following behind. I greeted him politely in the narrow lane, absolutely petrified of being within two feet of those huge supercilious-looking animals, then felt terribly 'village woman'-ish when they were safely past me.

Back by the river there was still no sign of spouting geysers, but it was only a matter of time, I was assured. Baba, Nabi, son and I sat in the shade for lunch. Nabi produced a twist of salt and Baba a knife; newspaper squares were our plates. A loaf of bread, a fist-sized lump of salty wet cheese, tomatoes and a large brown onion were placed in front of me. The tomatoes were no problem, the cheese was difficult, but the large onion was impossible, and after eating a quarter of the loaf of bread, I was forced to admit defeat. All three looked more worried than they had over the envisaged fountains. Any woman who couldn't put away such a modest-sized snack was obviously ailing. Baba had told Selim weeks ago that a woman as thin as me was useless. The sense of inadequacy the bread and onion remaining on our sack tablecloth bestowed on me was enormous, and my minor triumph of passing the camels melted under the weight of failure.

I left as the sun dipped behind the mountain. Nabi was going to work by hurricane lamp, as he was paid for the completed job rather than on a daily rate.

Next morning was cool and crisp with the leaves of the orange trees glistening in the sun and large puddles left by overnight rain straddled the track. Once again I was confident and happy. Over dinner the previous evening, Aydın had assured me that a pump and piping would be no problem. He would visit later in the day to inspect the hole. Walking through Baba's orchard, I could see Nabi, sonless, but with a companion even older than himself. Moving closer, I could see a look of quiet satisfaction on Baba's face as he watched proceedings from his kitchen chair.

Tentatively, I moved closer to our multi-sided 45-square-meter swimming pool. It was over a meter deep with Nabi's neat piles of rocks outside. It was dry....it was dry...it was dry...not even a puddle from the rains! Giving a bellow of joy, I did a clumsy jig, hopping around in my ill-fitting Wellington boots. Baba, Nabi and the newcomer laughed with me. "Allah is good," I was told. It was now time to start building the foundations.

CHAPTER 3.

MY DAYS SETTLED into a pleasant routine; walking to the house each morning, I began to recognise faces and put names to them. Ibrahim with his large grey horse was to be seen each day. Holding a rope tied to the bridle, he would stand and gaze into the distance as the horse devoured all it could reach over the garden fences. When an irate resident shouted abuse, Ibrahim would look surprised and drag the animal to the grassy verge. I would pass the *simit* man pedalling his rusting bicycle to the village centre and each morning he would stop and sell me one of the little bread rings heaped in the large glass case fixed to the handle bars. I would often meet Baba Macit taking his tractor for an airing. This far-from-new machine had been bought with some of the money kept in the safe at the bank. Having never strayed more than 40 miles from his orchard, he had taken a bus four times that distance to the town of Aydın's tractor fair. Following a quick lesson from the vendor in the art of tractor driving, he then proceeded to drive it all the way home on the verge of the highway. Sometimes he would use it to pull a plough between the trees in the orchard, but more often it was used to drive around the neighbourhood.

I spent hours cleaning the tiny rivulets bisecting the land and Nabi helped me arrange stepping stones to negotiate the larger stream between the bulldozed track and the land. On the days I stayed until dusk, tired and happy, I would wander back to Şahide's with a bunch of watercress gleaned from the edge of the river. House-bound on wet days, I would sit ensconced on a cushion as I plodded my way through Stanford Shaw's *History of the Ottoman Empire and Modern Turkey*. Solmaz and Aydın had a wonderful library with an impressive section in English; there was a feast of reading to fill future winter days and evenings.

Şahide worried about me; she arrived one morning to find me shoeless. She bodily threw me on a cushion and rushed to find slippers. With gestures and later a translation from Solmaz, she made me understand that going barefoot, even on carpet, was risking having the cold rush up from the ground to my head, which could kill me stone dead. A few days later, finding me sitting in the sun on the warm concrete doorstep, she dragged me off, explaining that cold zapping up one's bottom hole was even more lethal than unshod feet. She taught me to cover my sensible M&S knickers as they waved on the clothes line; masked by tea-towels, there was no risk of the local men being driven crazy with lust. We also had the problem of my scanty intake of food; she would bring me shopping bags full of vegetables, generous platters of rice and great lumps of cake. She knew of no sensible person who would eat a couple of slices of bread rather than devour a loaf.

On the evening of my birthday I felt lonely and pathetic. Being a bit of a drama queen, I stuck a candle in one of her wedges of cake and, sitting in the dark, sang "Happy Birthday" as the tears ran down my face. Having seen the flickering light from her kitchen, she arrived in a flurry to show me we were not experiencing one of the regular power cuts. Bewildered by the cake, candle and tears, she gathered me in her arms and rocked me like a baby. Early next morning Solmaz arrived, having been alerted that all was not well. After I had explained my wimpy behaviour, she invited me to dinner that evening and unbeknown to me rushed home to bake a birthday cake.

Each morning Ayşe the milk lady would deliver me a jar of warm fresh milk. Short, stout, long beyond her prime and smelling of cowshed, she would sometimes borrow a few liras from me to overcome a shortage of ready cash. These transactions were always extremely serious affairs as she insisted on laboriously writing out an IOU which would be ceremoniously torn up when the debt was repaid. Like most village women of her generation, her marriage had been arranged. She had fallen in love with a handsome young forestry worker. Unfortunately he was from the East and everyone knows that people from beyond the province borders are not to be trusted, let alone someone from so far away. A marriage to an older fisherman was quickly arranged, but a few months after the nuptials the new husband saw Ayşe meeting her love in the forest. With his manhood threatened, the bridegroom returned home for his gun and shot the handsome outsider dead. Fortunately the judge was a local man and understood the ways of village life; after only a few years in prison her husband was free to return to the bay and his fishing boat. Ayşe and her daughter continued to live in his little cottage and he, until his recent death, lived on his boat. Although shunned by her relatives and the village women, she had a sweet dreamy smile; her great love had not grown old or difficult - to her he was still that dashing young stranger from far away.

Dereköy is a new village. With the swampy river flats behind the beach, it had been a malaria area until concerted efforts in the late 1930's eradicated the anopheles mosquito from the bay. Tucked between the pine-clad mountains and the sea, the soil was rich and productive and villagers from further inland had taken advantage of the cheap land. At night I could hear the whistles of the forestry guards as they signalled to each other along the length of the forested peninsula that all was well.

The post office was the linchpin of the community. In the winter the men would move from the tea house to sit around the postmaster's stove and glean the latest news as they warmed their bones. The air in the room was always heavy and stifling hot, the smell of the heated stove pipes mingling with the aroma of damp coats and pungent Turkish cigarettes.

Ekrem Bey, the Postmaster, was lord of all he surveyed from behind his desk. His responsible position in the village weighed heavy on his shoulders and he always expected to be treated with the respect due to a man of such importance. If through some unfortunate incident one slighted him, merely buying a stamp could take forty minutes as he busied himself with more pressing issues. I was told that Mr. Bantam once had actually shouted at Ekrem Bey. A retired city man could not have been expected to realise the enormity of such foolishness, but for years he paid for his mistake. A short man who clucks and fusses, Mr Bantam left the city a failure, but arrived in the village ready to set himself up as leader of the community. Quickly nicknamed after a small fussy hen, he was at first tolerated and then ignored.

The post office had a tall long counter over which one's transactions took place. After the business of the visit was completed, the favoured would be invited around the back for tea and gossip. Taking up most of the back wall was the telephone switchboard, with its plugs and cables and, on the desk in front of the panel of numbered sockets, Ekrem Bey's headset. A buzzing sound was the signal for our postmaster to don his ear-phones and, guided by a white disk indicating which number was demanding his attention, with a flourish he would plug a cable into the socket. A conversation could last up to five minutes before a second plug would be connected to the number the caller had requested, followed by vigorous cranking of the handle at the side of the panel. Rarely did anyone request a call beyond the village boundaries; and if they did it usually indicated an emergency. More often than not, the single line to the outside world was out of order...rain, wind, lightning or fallen trees being blamed for these frequent failures.

This master of communications always listened to conversations between callers. Sometimes he would chip in with an opinion or observation; mainly he just sat quietly, nodding or shaking his head as he eavesdropped. There was nothing furtive about his behaviour and I never heard anyone complain. Nobody, it seemed, considered phone calls to be private conversations.

My name was on the waiting list for a telephone, but rarely was a line relinquished, so the hope of having my own socket and little white disk was somewhat futile. Every Friday morning I was at the post office by nine to wait for a call from Selim in Saudi Arabia. If the line was down or he failed to get through within an hour, I would return next day to wait again. To Ekrem Bey it was a personal challenge to get that call: if someone wanted to ring another village they were told the line was down, and if a call came through on that line, he would jump to answer it. If it was not for me, he would tell the caller that the party they wanted was not at home and to ring an hour later. When my call did come through, a long conversation would be conducted before I was allowed to speak to Selim. As we spoke in English, our postmaster could not be part of our conversation, so he would get all the news before I managed to get a word in. But I couldn't resent Ekrem Bey's hogging the phone: his triumphant joy was so genuine it seemed mean-spirited to think that these calls were mine alone.

Our cottage had the wooden framework and roof completed by the time the children and Selim arrived for Christmas. Our teenage daughter Saus joined in the spirit of things, helping me search Muğla for a turkey and fluttering her eyelashes at a forestry officer who was conned into presenting her with a pine branch suitable for Christmas decorations. One of the local schoolteachers fell head over heels in love with her pearly complexion and flame-red hair. He shadowed us at a distance every time we ventured out, but Saus was unimpressed. Both offspring put their seal of approval on the land, with Selim and our fifteen-year-old son Pog going about their manly business, checking on the construction site and exploring in a small and very old rowing boat bought as Pog's Christmas present.

Christmas day the heavens opened, and buckets to catch the drips dotted the floor. Somehow between school and Heathrow both offspring had made a detour, and smart green bags containing Christmas pud, crackers and a multitude of goodies were produced. To me it was a wonderful season of good cheer, and as I waved them off next day I was already planning our next family gathering. The children were flying back to England and Selim was returning to Saudi to ship our household goods and join me permanently.

I am glad I was unaware of just how long it would be before the four of us would be together again.

CHAPTER 4.

THE BUILDING OF the house was put on hold 'til spring. Selim was having problems. The Prince he worked for had spent most of his money on his football team. Not only were back wages not forthcoming, but he decided he wanted Selim to stay. To work in Saudi one has to have a sponsor who arranges an entry visa; unfortunately, it is a country where one also must have an exit visa. To the spoiled little princeling it was simple...he instructed his office not to supply an exit visa, and my Turk was well and truly stuck. Only those who have lived in Saudi can relate to such Lewis Carroll scenarios. Hopefully, with tact and patience Selim would sort things out.

Soon spring arrived and along with the storks, herons and kingfishers, the builders returned to continue constructing the cottage. It was more than a month before I realised why the work was continuing in fits and starts. The building team had taken on a lucrative contract to build a house 25 miles away in Marmaris at the same time as they finished ours. I waited for Selim to arrive and sort things out; it was only towards the end of May that Aydın stepped in to take charge, and suddenly, like magic, the walls began to grow. A chimney specialist came from Muğla to build the fireplace and a glazier from a nearby village fitted the window panes.

Aydın was due to drive Solmaz and me to the Muğla market one Thursday when he decided we might have to cancel plans for an outing that day. The tiler had arrived and, though the contractor insisted he was the master tiler of the Orient, Aydın wondered if having only one eye might affect his workmanship. After checking on progress an hour later, he returned with the news that the man was brilliant; it was a pleasure to watch him tile the bathroom walls. Early in the building process, we had learnt that nothing could be taken for granted. Without constant patrols, the workers would make the concrete with too little cement. A nasty altercation over the rationing of reinforcing rods had blighted the atmosphere for days.

We enjoyed our trip to Muğla and returned to admire the bathroom. The walls were beautiful. But the floor...each tile, grouted perfectly, tilted in a different direction. Our man was the maestro of the vertical, but the horizontal was not his forte. The contractor blustered; Baba said it was the shadows of the afternoon sun that made things look wrong. While they gazed at this optical illusion, I brought a bucket of water from the stream and threw it over the floor. Twenty or thirty small puddles appeared, with a mini pond in the far corner. The contractor, beaten, was forced to have the floor redone.

Before the building was complete, we found that the fireplace didn't draw, and smoke billowed into the room. This, we were told, was because of the trees; you can't have a functional fireplace in a forest. Use a gas heater, said the foreman. It took much adrenaline and many heated words, but we have the only fireplace in the world which, in spite of trees, draws smoke up its chimney.

The doorstep was so steep that one had to take a run before leaping. Many deep discussions and demonstration leaps later, a second step was built.

The problems went on and on, and we ignored some of the oddities. The battle of words was too exhausting; it was easier to leave it and remedy it later ourselves. The kitchen flooring extending out into the salon was not ignored; the unlevelled window frames caused a week-long war, with Aydın prowling, armed with a spirit level. One feature remains: a half bent eight-inch nail protrudes from the kitchen door frame. I have varnished it and will not have it removed. I have a theory that it is the modern equivalent of a keystone. Remove it and the whole house will fold like a pack of cards.

By mid-July, all was finished bar electricity; sheaves of papers were filled in after The Aunt grudgingly sent her power of attorney from Istanbul. Power poles were erected along the track and after a week of waiting, the electricity department came and strung wires. A 100-gallon tank was placed on a stand by the river with a small electric pump to fill it. Drinking water I could get from the public fountain in the village square.

I waited for my weekly phone-call from Selim to ask his advice about the woodwork. It was a particularly bad line that day and he had to shout his reply twice before I understood. He was emphatic that it must all be treated with two coats of boiling linseed oil.

I bought a four-gallon tin of the stuff and slowly man-handled it down the track and over the stream. I filled a two-pint saucepan and put it to heat on the little gas stove the builders had used for tea making; the smell was so dreadful that I had to move the stove into the garden. Up the ladder balancing the hot saucepan, I brushed it on the eaves and whenever the oil cooled I would reheat it to ensure that the job was done as Selim would like. The oil just disappeared into the wood and it took me a week of hard work to give the doors, window frames, ceilings, shutters and eaves two coats. The smell was overpowering and the oil burned my hands and stuck in my hair. The large tin had proved insufficient and I had to haul a second tin all the way from the road. Next time I spoke to Selim he suggested another coat when I told him how the wood had soaked up the oil. Eventually the job was finished but it was weeks before the smell abated and I could walk inside without feeling ill.

When Selim eventually arrived from Saudi he was most impressed by the job I had done on the woodwork. I told him of the saucepan and how I had conscientiously reheated the oil. He couldn't believe that I had balanced on a rickety ladder with a pot of boiling oil. Then he explained why he was amazed: his directions had been "boiled linseed oil." I now know that one can buy the stuff raw or boiled, although the boiled is considered superior. Boiling oil has proved even better: in 14 years the cottage has never needed another coat.

His sister having flown to Saudi to see her father and Selim, Pog arrived alone for the summer holidays, just in time for my move from Şahide's to our very own cottage. Mehmet, the lemon tree donor, arrived with his tractor, and with the neighbours, helped us heap all our accumulated possessions into the trailer. With our friends waving goodbye as if we were moving to distant shores, I balanced on the tractor mudguard in the time-honoured village woman fashion, while Pog sat atop the motley load. At the stepping-stone end of our track, halting with a lurch, our driver went off to round up some muscle to help with the heavy items. While he was gone, we carted the lighter stuff across the stream, leaving the large fridge and oven to be manhandled by Mehmet and the two Kurdish labourers he had hijacked.

By sunset we had everything installed and, having eaten our first meal cooked in the new kitchen and feeling tired but smug, we settled down to read and listen to BBC World Service. Not long after dark we heard a crashing in the reeds near the bedroom window. We switched off the radio and light, listening in silence to the strange noises and cracking of reed stems. Peering out the windows, we seemed to be surrounded by shadows moving in the moon-light. Which were from the eucalyptus branches and which were our tormentors, we couldn't tell. The door was locked but the sash windows as yet had no clasps, and no way were we going to open the windows to close and lock the shutters. As at any moment they could burst in, Pog armed himself with the carving knife and steak hammer. I pretended to be brave, as a mother should, and Pog as man of the house did a good job of masking his fear. What seemed like hours later, we heard splashing on the river bank followed by silence; our aggressors probably growing bored with their game, had left by boat. We felt betrayed by the locals who had never shown us anything but kind-ness; Pog suggested I would be safer at Sahide's when he returned to school and I was not slow to agree.

Solmaz and Aydın were away in Istanbul, so waking late next morning following a night of little sleep with no-one to turn to for advice, we prepared ourselves for war. To bolster our courage we both agreed it was hardly likely there would be a repeat performance, but just in case, we intended to be ready. Pog closed all the shutters while I collected fist-size rocks for ammunition. Venturing to the village for bread and torch batteries, we scanned the faces of the locals, trying to identify likely suspects. On the way home we collected a pile of empty raki bottles left at a picnic area, and as evening drew close we arranged the bottles with our extensive arsenal of ammunition. Late in the afternoon Pog tied nylon fishing-line from tree to tree at chest height, to hamper the enemy hordes. By dusk we were nailed, shuttered and securely locked in.

It had been dark less than an hour when we heard the first sounds of unwelcome guests. With the moon partially hidden behind a cloud it was difficult to see through the latticed shutters, but with our heads pressed against the glass we could make out someone crawling on hands and knees towards the window. Directly beneath us he seemed to be scrabbling in the wood stacked against the house. With a display of bravery I still find hard to believe, Pog shone the torch down towards the woodpile, then shrieked with laughter. He seemed hysterical and it was sometime before he could gasp, "Pig...wild pig." It may have been common knowledge to one and all that wild boar often swam across the river from the plain at the end of the bay, but it was certainly news to us. Giddy with relief, we toasted our bravery with cooking sherry, becoming gigglier by the glass.

Within days Pog announced there was a rat in the roof. How long the rat and I would have shared lodgings was anyone's guess, but my deafness would have given it plenty of time to make a home. Once alerted by sharper ears than mine, I laid down rat poison and the problem was forgotten after a few days.

At the post office one morning, Ekrem gave me the message that the *vali* and his family were planning to visit me that afternoon. Now, the *vali* is an extremely important person, the governor of the whole province, and it was a great honour that he was going to visit. I rushed home to bake cakes, while Pog tried to sort out seating arrangements. Our little sitting area, cosy with two, was a bit of a squash with three, so there was no way we could entertain such illustrious guests inside. As yet there was no garden furniture, so Pog arranged cushions on a large kilim spread under the trees and placed my large brass tray on a log from the firewood pile. The finished effect was very eastern looking.

In the tiny kitchen I managed to produce a thing vaguely related to an apple strudel and, with a stroke of luck, a marvellous looking chocolate cake. A leftover piece of pastry was used to make cheese straws; glasses, cups and saucers were polished and the sugar tongs located. We were spruced up and all was ready by mid-afternoon.

At 4:30 we heard our guests making their way down the track from the road and my brave and gallant son stood in the stream to assist the ladies across the stepping stones. Mr. Governor and his two teenage children spoke fluent English; Mrs. Governor didn't but was charming about my hesitant, pathetic attempts at Turkish. They viewed the cottage extensively, with so much interest that we used up a whole five minutes. However nice guests are, a cottage smaller than the average Turkish salon doesn't take much time to admire.

While the adults settled themselves on the cushions, the three young people went off to explore the river in Pog's boat. All was going rather well, I thought. My guests asked about my husband's family. Which branch was he from? Which twig on the branch? Where was he born, and so forth. The Ottoman side clarified, we then moved to the famous Pasha on the other side and, having established just who was who and where Selim fitted on that tree, I was told once again the story of the battle of Plevne.

Nearly everyone I meet gets great pleasure in telling me of this historic battle. Hardly anyone stops to think that as my surname is the same as this famous general's, I just might have heard the story before. No matter, my guests were happy. When the young people returned, I served tea as Pog busied himself with plates and cakes.

Relaxed now, with the visit an obvious success, I was jolted out of my smug mood by Mrs. Governor's high-pitched scream. Turning to see what her shaking finger was pointing at, I saw it. The damned rat had chosen the middle of my tea party to die. Did it die as any normal rat would? Just curl up in the roof and quietly expire? Oh, no. My rat had to take a leap from the eaves and now lay twitching only a yard from the edge of the kilim. I acted shocked and horrified and tried to divert attention from the wretched rodent, hoping Pog could whisk the body away and I could smooth things over with another cup of tea. No such luck. That rat was going to get its money's worth before making its final exit. With a feeble squeak, it staggered to its feet, moved forward a few inches and then collapsed on its side. Valiantly, with pathetic whimpers, it struggled onto all fours and moved forward again, hamming it up in the best tradition of the old movies. He reminded me of those cow-boys who, with ten bullets in their bodies, could fall and roll about groaning for a full two minutes before subsiding. That rat must have rolled, twitched and staggered for longer than any Hollywood cowboy.

In the end I took a leaf out of Hollywood's book myself, and did a full, "Oh-I'm-a-city-girl-and-this-is-all-too-much-for-me" routine. The *vali* helped me, weeping, into the house, while his wife busied herself making a new pot of tea. Everyone marvelled at my bravery in living alone, so far from the village, and assured me that having a rat leap out of the roof was not a reflection on my housekeeping. At this point the rodent, deprived of an audience, belatedly did the decent thing and quietly died.

Gathering up their possessions, Mr. and Mrs. Governor took their leave, thanking me for a wonderful afternoon as Pog escorted them across the stream and up the track and I clung weakly to the gate until they had disappeared from sight.

Later, as we collected up the cups and saucers, Pog gave me a long hard look. None of his mates' mothers, he commented, could have upstaged a dying rat. I took it as a compliment.

CHAPTER 5.

BY NOVEMBER WINTER had arrived. The first savage winds found the gaps between the windows and frames, sending currents hurling through the cottage to make the fireplace smoke and the candle flame flicker. The rains, so ferocious that gutters and downpipes are useless, hurl from the wide eaves like a waterfall. Imagine a cloudburst that lasts for days and you have the general idea of Dereköy rain. Clouds, huge and black, charge from opposing sides of the bay, hell-bent on ramming each other. The crashes of thunder make the little cottage thud and tremble while the lightning illuminates the mountains and plain. For sometimes more than a week, the battles rage with rarely a pause for breath.

Within the first hours of a storm, the electricity was always cut, sometimes for days, but with gas for cooking and a supply of candles, the only problem was the water tank. I became obsessed about the tank running dry, keeping it topped up whenever there was electricity. Perhaps it was a reaction to the lavatory at Şahide's with its unorthodox flush that made me neurotic about a constant water supply.

When the rains stopped there would be several days of clear cloudless skies, the sky so blue and the hills so verdant, it looked like a picture on the lid of a cheap chocolate box. This was the time to trek up to the village; squelching through the muddy lanes in my wellies, I would collect fir cones brought down by the storms. Having replenished my food stocks and caught up on gossip at the post office, I would trudge home to start my post-storm chores. Firstly, the tank had to be filled as soon as there was electricity, drinking water supplies replenished and the streams and rivulets cleared of debris. The woodpile needed to be checked, with perhaps more cone excursions to top up supplies. If the tarpaulin on the little boat had slipped, there would be an energetic bailing stint which did wonders for the stomach muscles.

For a few days the village came to life again. The fishing boats headed out into the bay and the village was adorned with banners of washing. Chain-saws droned in the distance as the forestry workers cleared broken branches and fallen trees. The teahouse with its steam-shrouded windows would be full to bursting as the men caught up on every snippet of gossip. There was usually a car accident to discuss. City slickers with too much power under the bonnet barrel down the dual-carriageway above the village and are prone to fly off the side of the mountain.

For me the most important thing was that the predicted flooding didn't occur: whatever deluge Thor's thunderclaps throw at the cottage, all quickly drains away. The streams move from gurgle to gush and the river to an impressive torrent, but the cottage stands aloof without even a puddle on the bottom step.

In late November I flew to England to spend some time with Saus, who was now attending college in London. Her father had found her a flat without me being involved in the decision and I wasn't quite ready to accept that my baby girl, at 18, was capable of looking after herself. It was the winter the British Government conducted an intensive campaign to educate the public about the dangers of AIDS. Umpteen times a day there were AIDS awareness ads on telly, and several times a week there were very frank discussions between panels of experts. Before viewing these pro-grammes, I would have said I was well informed and quite broadminded. I certainly wasn't.

During one such discussion, a kindly looking blue-rinse granny said, "And of course it is obvious the risk taken by people who play water sports." Well, it might have been obvious to her and the rest of the panellists nodding wisely, but it certainly wasn't to me. As both children were going to spend the Christmas break with their father in Saudi, I started to worry. They spent most of the day in the swim-ming pool and often, with a net across the pool, two teams would play a noisy game with shuttlecocks and bats. With much jumping and splashing, that surely qualified as a water sport. (I'd already deleted yachting and windsurfing from my danger list.)

Immediately I telephoned my ex-husband and with much concern, related what I'd heard; perhaps more chlorine in the swimming pool would be the answer, I suggested. There was a long silence on the line before he gently told me that this was not what the sweet-looking old lady had in mind and that there was no need to worry about the children playing boisterous games in the pool. "What did she mean?" I asked. "Talk to one of your sophisticated friends," he said.

Over the next few days I found my sophisticated friends as clueless as myself, but eventually I and half a dozen others were enlightened. Apart from being stunned, I was dismayed at the huge gap in my sex education. What else didn't I know?

A few months later, home in the village, lulled by the quiet, uncomplicated way of life, I forgot about the concerns of the so-called civilised world. Waiting one morning for a bus, I was joined by an earnest young man who spoke English. He was working in the village, he told me. "Doing what?" I asked. "I from the University of Ankara am," he said. "To be researching," he added. Wow, here is something interesting, I thought. "What are you researching?" "I am the research doing of the honey of the penis." Honey of the penis, blimey! Another great gap in my education! "You the honey of the penis are knowing?" he enquired. "Oh! Yes. Yes," I said, trying to look very worldly and all-knowing. "This area of Turkey famous is for the honey of the penis." "Yes. Yes," I managed to repeat as I tried not to gabble. This can't be happening, I thought, I must be going mad; or maybe he's mad. Thank God the bus was coming, but it seemed to be taking an age to come down the hill. I couldn't keep this up much longer. As the bus stopped and I rushed to the steps he said, "Of course, it's not all penis." "Please, God, save me," I prayed. "It only honey of *Penis Brutia* is," he said. Enlightenment flooded through me as I stumbled to a seat. He meant *pinus*, Latin for pine. Beehives placed close to our forest when the pines are in flower produce a much-acclaimed honey, but I had thought it was only well known locally.

"You must try our village honey," I advise visitors. "It's famous all over Turkey."

In the following spring, one of the fields between my cottage and the village began to fill with beehives. Each year the itinerant beekeepers, with their tents and sky-blue hives stacked on the back of ageing trucks, descend on the village as the pines come into flower. Each morning I'd see more hives and angry, unsettled bees as I walked to the village for my bread.

One morning, on opening my front door, I was stung by nine bees before I had even started down the steps. Back indoors, dabbing garlic juice on the reddening blotches, I saw large numbers of angry bees buzzing around the house and garden.

Setting off to the village draped in my Saudi abaya and veils, I hurried along the lane, totally shrouded from the irate insects. Reaching the field, I could see the hives that yesterday had been stacked two deep had turned overnight into multi-storey condominiums.

In the safety of the village, I hid my robe and veils in my basket and made my way to the *muhtar*, standing outside the teahouse, desperate to relate the trauma I had suffered. Usually a kind man, Kemal Bey was rather brusque. Rolling his eyes with exasperation, he said, "They are always angry when they first arrive. They'll settle down in a week or two."

Almost in tears, I scuttled home, replacing my bee-proof garb once I was out of sight of the villagers. By afternoon the novelty of the poor-me episode had worn thin. I vowed to be sensible, return to the village, stock up with provisions and settle down to a few days writing letters. I could even get stuck into those rather dry volumes of Ottoman history.

Once more hiding my robes as I reached the village, I made my way over the crest of the small but steep hill. Over the brow, I could see there was much excitement in the village square. Four large army trucks stood outside the teahouse. In the vehicles I could see helmeted soldiers in khaki, all clutching guns. Two officers with a mass of gold braid were talking to three of the village councillors.

Moving towards the bakery, I met Aydın Bey coming out of the *muhtar's* office. Seeing me, he rushed over and enquired if I was all right. As I started to relate my bee problem, he stopped me by saying he knew all about it, but asked how many times I had been stung. When I said nine, his face did not change but his eyes started to twinkle. He insisted I get into his car and go with him to see Solmaz. On the way, I asked him what the military presence was all about, but he refused to tell me, muttering that my laughing in front of the villagers was the last thing he needed. On reaching the house, he told his wife to forget about tea and to join us in the salon.

With a great hoot of laughter he banged his hands on the table; tears streamed down his face. This was quite overwhelming; Aydın is not a man given to raucous laughter. Between snorts and chuckles the story came out.

Our *muhtar*, Kemal Bey, is a member of the rightist party, while Naci, who had overheard my morning conversation with the *muhtar*, is an active member of the leftist party. Always eager to score points, Naci had contacted his party headquarters in the provincial capital to report that ninety bees had stung the foreign wife of an important Turk and the *muhtar* had dismissed her in an abrupt and abusive manner. News of the scandal was passed on to the governor of the province, who in turn alerted the Gendarme. Somewhere between our zealous Naci's phone call and the military intervention, I had become the wife of the President of the Republic's best friend and the number of stings was approaching nine hundred.

The hives were to be removed immediately, by the soldiers if necessary. Aydın had been called to convey to me, in English, the humble apologies of our poor brow- beaten *muhtar* and to pass on to me the governor's card. I was to call the Governor's office if I had the slightest problem. My friend, though worried I was lying alone in the cottage almost dead, had convinced the authorities that the bees should not be moved. He felt angry itinerant beekeepers might prove a greater problem than bees. The governor decreed that in the future no hives were to be placed within the boundaries of the village.

In the following years governors have come and gone; our own Kemal Bey has retired. But still no beehive can be found within the village precincts.

Following the bee adventure I spent a week playing tourist in Istanbul and, ready to return to village life, I booked a seat on the twice-weekly flight to Dalaman. The flight was repeatedly delayed but, being half way through a compelling book, I was quite happy to have the opportunity to sit and read. Eventually, an announcement informed us that free refreshments were being served.

I was in no hurry to join the line of passengers waiting for complimentary tea and biscuits, so I had my nose in my book when a well-dressed businessman interrupted my thoughts to explain to me in faultless English that I was entitled to sustenance. I thanked him, explaining that I had understood the announcement and he left to join the queue. An hour later and we were still waiting; by this time I had been engaged in conversation by a middle-aged Turkish couple. With their basic English and my less than basic Turkish, we were saved from our torturous conversation by a charming young man who had attended university in the UK. Time passed quickly and at midnight we boarded our plane. In a little over an hour we were safely on the Dalaman runway.

In those days, Dalaman Airport's terminal consisted of two large sheds, one clearly marked IN and the other OUT. I hasten to add that these signs were large and in both Turkish and English; there might not have been all the latest trappings of an international airport but nothing could be clearer. Flights were few and far between and one had to walk a few hundred yards from the plane to the IN shed.

Struggling towards the arrival barn with my customary overweight in-flight bag and all the extra bits and pieces I'd accumulated, I was met by the middle-aged businessman who was waiting for me halfway across the tarmac.

Thinking he had stopped to help me with my parcels, I couldn't believe my ears when he told me that it was far too late for me to continue my journey to Marmaris. It would be better if I spent the night in a hotel with him and resumed my journey in the morning. To make his intentions quite clear, he then tried to embrace me, parcels and all. Very coldly, I told him that I didn't think it was a very good idea at all and as I moved away he called out, "I was going to buy you a meal."

As I entered the arrivals shed laughing at his audacity, the young university graduate was waiting for me. He was concerned that the businessman might have annoyed me. Still laughing, I explained to him that I had just found out my value on the open market. He was not amused, but clearly horrified. I explained that it didn't matter and that it was really very funny, but he took it as a slur on the manners of all Turkish men.

He carried my bag and bundles to the baggage area and insisted that he drive me home. As he was heading in the opposite direction, the drive would add at least two hours to his trip. He was so upset that in the end it seemed easiest to accept his gracious offer.

All the way to the village he apologised on behalf of the entire Turkish nation and explained over and over again that some ignorant men thought that all foreign women were of dubious "moral inclination."

Escorting me down the last 200 yards of narrow track on foot, loaded down with all my gear, he shook my hand formally at the door and disappeared into the night. I have never seen him since.

The one and only village taxi driver had by this time

become an important person in my life. Ahmet has nine gold teeth, a sign of wealth amongst the older villagers. He has a dynamic, short, roly-poly wife who berates him loudly and publicly if she catches him drinking raki. He always looks chastened and ashamed when he's being shouted at, but he never answers back or gives her a thump, as one would expect. His clothes appear to have been borrowed from a larger man and, as he only visits the village barber once a week, his face always sports a stiff grey stubble.

His ancient Opel, although tired and dented, was polished daily as it sat in the village square ready for business. Ahmet could be found at any time of the day in the teahouse or the post office. Between them, he and the Postmaster knew all that went on in the area.

If a week went by without me getting a call from Selim, Ahmet would drive me the twenty-odd miles to the nearest international telephone, where I could put a call through to Saudi Arabia. Hunched over the wheel, he drove at speeds that made the doors rattle and the engine thump. He insisted on speaking English, refusing to listen if I tried Turkish. We were often at cross purposes, as his English vocabulary was limited to a dozen or so words. It was really much easier to have the same conversation each trip and I learned not to introduce new subjects or observations for fear we would zoom over a cliff-like drop. Each trip he pointed out the landmarks, turning his head and flashing his wonderful teeth as the car careened across the road.

We usually passed the camel man with his two beasts, plodding homeward at the end of a day's work. "Orhan's chamils," he says, and each time I exclaim with surprise. We pass the Byzantine water dome and he points out the new communal water tap that had replaced it. Süleyman the Magnificent's fort was commented on as we sped by and I wished my Turkish was up to telling him about the collapsed tunnel the children and I had found at the foot of its crumbling walls. I wanted to tell him it was originally a Genoese

-53-

trading castle, that was rebuilt as a marine fort in 1520 AD and used as a staging post for the Ottoman military when they sailed forth to conquer the islands of Cos, Simi and Rhodes. Just past the fort was the so-called 'Arab Cemetery' where the slaves from the days of the huge cotton plantations were buried. The few descendants of these people living in the area look to be of distinctly African heritage, so the cemetery's name is puzzling. Further on, we pass the 4th-century BC Carian tombs. There were a lot more, but there was scant recognition of such things when the high road was built, and only three remain.

As we reached the cross-roads and junction with the main highway, Ahmet always slowed the vehicle to a crawl, then a stop. Turning towards me, he would enquire, "Istanbul?" This being the signal for me to look horrified and shout, "No, no! Marmaris...Marmaris, please!" Each trip I looked suitably worried that he thought I wanted to set out on the 500-mile trip to Istanbul. Lowering his head onto the steering wheel, he shook with laughter. Turning to look at my face set him off on a new bout of merriment. I have never known if the joke was so exquisite that it was just as funny each time Ahmet tricked me, or if it was the thought that I was as thick as two short planks and repeatedly fell into the trap that was so hilarious.

CHAPTER 6.

BY LATE SPRING I was heavily into the food smuggling trade. As the locals' crops matured I was inundated with generous gifts. Crates of tomatoes, sacks of cucumbers, kilos of peppers along with eggplants, lettuces and marrows would be left on my doorstep hours before I woke in the morning. Brought up in the years of rationing following the Second World War, to waste food is unthinkable. After a bout of bottling and pickle making, I had enough preserves to stave off famine, but still the gifts arrived. Solmaz and Aydın didn't welcome the idea of me donating these goods to them. They were already surrounded by a glut of produce themselves.

Baba Macit monitored my activities too closely for me to enrich the compost heap with these gifts, and the eucalyptus roots made it impossible for me to dig holes big enough to quietly dispose of anything larger than a radish.

Eventually I started to pack my suitcase with produce every time I was going into Marmaris. Ahmet never questioned my habit of lugging a heavy bag each time I went to town to make a phone call. The lads who had befriended me at one of the carpet shops were only too happy to dispose of the kilos of wonderful village vegetables...while I could look my neighbours in the eye as I told them how much their gifts were appreciated.

One morning while ensconced on the post office steps as I awaited my phone-call, I saw a beautiful white horse coming down the hill towards me. The few horses in the village tend to be small and sway-backed with dull shaggy coats. This was a storybook steed, put on earth to save damsels from black knights. The rider was not wearing armour but was dressed immaculately and shod in beautiful riding boots. As they halted at the steps I squinted up at the rider when he spoke to me in English. Jeremy James had arrived in Dereköy the previous evening and was riding from Turkey to Offa's Dyke in Wales, a trek he seemed to think was a perfectly normal thing to do. We walked to the cottage together where his horse Ahmed Paşa could feast on fresh grass. Amongst my mail that morning was a letter from Pog's school containing his school report. As we sat in the salon waiting for the water to boil for coffee, I asked Jeremy if he minded me reading my mail. On seeing the mono-gram on the envelope he gasped with surprise...he had for years lived in Gloucestershire near the school and knew many members of staff. Pog's house master was a drinking pal. We sat and stared at each other in silent amazement. In a Turkish village not even marked on the map I had invited home for coffee someone who actually drank with the awesome Mr. King.

For the next few days Jeremy and Ahmed Paşa would arrive for breakfast each morning and we would spend the day relating past adventures or visiting Marmaris to find a new saddle bag. Baba Macit watched us unrelentingly, seating himself on the tree stump by the cottage door and timing our excursions beyond the village. Baba knew that men and women don't have friendships without a drop of hanky-panky and, even if we had been so inclined, Baba's glowering presence would have saved the family honour.

Too soon it was time for Jeremy to move on towards Wales and I waved them goodbye as they disappeared through the neighbour's citrus orchard. I have never met them since, but Jeremy mentions our meeting in his book. A year later I thought I saw Ahmed Paşa in a village beyond Izmir but dismissed it as impossible. Once I had read *Saddletramp*, I was not so sure.

It was now over a year since I had seen Selim. Friends were disturbed and the villagers distressed. While some wondered how long it would take me to wake up to the fact that I had been deserted, others marvelled that I could patiently wait so long. At no stage did I realise just how long this farce could continue; like a reformed alcoholic I just got through each day one at a time.

In the salon a cigar sat on an ashtray; Selim's jacket was draped over a chair and a boating magazine sat on the table. Each morning I smoothed his dressing gown and placed it neatly at the foot of the bed. With his belongings around me, it gave the illusion that he was close, due to come in the door at any time. To give some focus to each day, I wrote lists of chores and things to do, assiduously crossing each completed trivial task off the list.

When the moon was full I would sit on the tree stump to gaze at the mountains and the silvery river. When Selim and I had become engaged I had given him a painting I had done. He gave me the full moon and promised it would appear every month for the rest of my life. Each month the full moon acted as a catalysis as I sat and wept at my impotency in the face of our bizarre situation. Drained and exhausted, I would go to bed, to wake next morning renewed for another month. The word lunar is twinned with insanity, but to me it was a monthly dose of therapy. Renewed, I would return to my lists, the company of BBC World Service and life in the village.

That was the spring that Can Bey died. We had met when Selim and I had first come to the village. He had retired from his consular post in Germany and he was supervising the building of his and his wife's dream home. Verrin had one year of service to complete before she could join him.

They had bought two plots of land to give them space around their house and the plans, although drawn up in Germany, had allowed every consideration to the Mediterranean climate: large rooms with expanses of glass overlooking the sea and the mountains beyond, wide eaves that would give shade from the heat of the day. For years they had made their plans, with every aspect thought out again and again.

Whilst I was having a few hiccups with the building of our small cottage, Can Bey was confronted by daunting problems. The local contractors had never built such a house and there were continual major obstacles to be overcome. The costs were soaring and a lesser man would have given up, but Can Bey plodded on. Long after I had moved into my cottage their house was at last finished. Verrin Hanim arrived; the furniture was chosen and their belongings from Munich unpacked.

One day a year later, whilst helping the gardener, Can Bey suffered a massive heart attack. It was said that he was dead before he fell to the ground. Verrin was devastated and, numb with shock, she just sat twisting her fingers in her lap as her friends tried to comfort her.

After the funeral, she sat pale and unspeaking as friends and villagers called to pay their respects.

One of the locals who had worked on the building of her

house kissed her hand respectfully and said, "Verrin Hanim, last night Can Bey visited me in a dream. He said that I was to tell you that you are to give me your second piece of land."

Verrin's hands stopped twitching and, looking up with a gentle smile, she said, "I'm so glad you brought it up. You see, Can came to me in a dream also, just before dawn. He said I was to tell you that he is very sorry but he's changed his mind."

The villagers had a way of watching, of knowing, of unity. They might barely tolerate each other at times, but they were as one in their mistrust of outsiders. News appeared to sometimes travel by osmosis. Most outsiders considered the locals to be fools, and the villagers seemed quite content to accept this description of themselves. Admittedly, some of the old timers didn't read or write, but Ekrem Bey in the post office helped them with any letter they received or needed to send. Naci, at the teahouse, read out bits from the newspaper, and the *muhtar* used the mosque loudspeaker to remind us of any taxes we must pay. The *muhtar* enjoyed the loudspeaker so much that even the shepherds in the far hills could hear his messages.

The morning the city man came was an ordinary spring morning. The women, bent over the tomato plants in the lower fields, saw the white Mercedes as it glided down the mountain road. The men, facing the road as they played cards at the teahouse, saw too. Those with their backs towards the road heard the car stop; interest quickened, but the heads stayed low over the cards.

We'd all seen the car before; last month it had cruised through the village, down the lanes and side roads. Osman Bey had seen its four occupants get out and walk up and down old Ibrahim's field on the hill. They had ignored Osman Bey, who had heard them use phrases like "one-hundred-bed capacity", "spectacular vista" and "cheap land" as they gazed at the bay below.

The city man sat himself at a spare table under the plane tree and ordered tea. Everyone waited, hunched over their cards. Hussein, the shoeshine boy, banged his brushes together and clattered his jars. Mehmet from the fruit stall wandered across the road and joined a table of older men playing backgammon. Those who could see the road listened to the approach of the second car. Those who couldn't see, didn't look. Everyone knew it would be Kemal Bey, the *muhtar*, alerted by the postmaster across the square. Ekrem had been cranking the handle of the party line even before the Mercedes had stopped.

Kemal Bey greeted the tables of players as he moved towards the stranger. He made a jovial display of welcome as he ordered tea. After a few minutes of muttered conversation, Kemal Bey called two of the older men to join him. He introduced Ömer Bey from Ankara and explained - just loud enough for all to hear - that Ömer Bey wanted to buy land in the area. The piece of land he was interested in was the field by the old fort.

"Does anyone know who the field belongs to?" asked the *muhtar*. Everybody knows who owns everything in the village, but it took much pondering to remember that Aslan's father owned that piece of land. Ömer Bey hinted that, if he could get the land at a reasonable price, he had a business venture in mind that would change the village and bring jobs.

The city man looked assured and sly. He asked if someone could possibly find Aslan and his father. The card players nodded approval at this quick-wittedness, while Ahmet made his way to his taxi. Kemal Bey ordered more tea as everybody waited for Ahmet to return with the landowner and son. The prayer call rang out, but nobody moved. The few ancients who prayed on weekdays would leave it until later.

When Ahmet eventually returned, it took some

manoeuvring to get old Ibrahim out of the vehicle. Usually a sprightly soul, he was enjoying his role in the proceedings. How long he'd had the news of the stranger in town was anybody's guess. Ömer Bey tried not to look impatient, but all could hear him cracking his knuckles as the old man was half-dragged to the table by his son.

Ibrahim didn't think he wanted to sell the land. No, he didn't use it for anything much, but it had belonged to his father. Kemal Bey excused himself, explaining that he didn't get involved in business deals. A few more chairs were dragged up to the table under the shady tree as the discussion continued.

An hour passed; Aslan was getting quite angry with his father, who, in the end, under an onslaught of advice, shrugged defeat. Ömer Bey had offered such a huge sum of money that, mistaking the stunned silence for horror at his meanness, he added another forty percent to the figure. It was explained to old Ibrahim that Ömer Bey was in a hurry to return to Ankara, so Aslan was sent off to find the title deed.

Half an hour later the Mercedes and the village taxi made their way up the mountain to the large town, where the land registry office would complete the formalities. The pertinent officials had been warned by Ekrem at the post office of the impending arrival, and the manager of the local bank had delayed his lunch. The stamping of the documents and paying of the transfer tax was over in minutes, and the bank manager was happy to deposit the cheque in an account newly opened for Ibrahim.

Ömer Bey was smiling, and very pleased with his day's work; he knew he had a bargain. Ahmet, the taxi driver, was smiling at the generous tip the new landowner had pressed on him. Ibrahim and Aslan showed no emotion, but they and the village looked forward to the day when the city man discovered that one can't build a hut, let alone a hotel, on land deemed as a water catchment for the village.

CHAPTER 7

EACH YEAR IN May the villagers would count the days as we waited for the windy moonlit night, knowing that our arsonist would strike. The forestry workers would vow that this time they would catch him. Villagers would not venture into the forest alone in case a fire started and they had no alibi. In spite of the vigilance of the forest guards, the fire would always start in an area not too far from the Forestry Department's headquarters. It was never in a part of the forest difficult to reach and all of us would turn out to watch the fire trucks race from the depot and the outlying villages. Men would climb trees with chain-saws to lop over-hanging branches and trucks overflowing with fire-fighters armed with shovels would arrive from other villages. Teams with copper backpacks would move in line dousing the embers. Senior forestry officers would direct the workers to various strategic positions and the air was full of smoke and the shouts of those in charge of operations. Mothers would shriek at their children, and amidst the tension and drama there was an almost festive air. We locals would stand in excited groups exchanging theories on why it happened every year and rehash the stories of earlier fires. It had been a regular event for years, so it couldn't be the lads of the town. Or maybe it wasn't the same person each year. If it was an outsider, how come he wasn't seen arriving in the village?

This year when the gusting wind grew stronger, the fire raced through the camping ground, burning several tents. Campers fleeing in their cars caused a traffic jam, with people panicking and screaming. The governor arrived from Muğla in a long black car and next day we featured in the Istanbul newspapers.

As we made our way home in groups, we were not aware that this was our arsonist's swan-song. The next year we all waited for the first full moon of the summer and the forestry staff was as usual poised for action. The moon waxed and waned, but there was no fire. June came and we all wondered if he would strike. He didn't, and our annual fire became a thing of the past. Sometimes in early spring the talk in the teahouse will turn to our arsonist, and the various theories about him will be aired once again. Some think he has left the district; others say he was a forestry worker who has retired. One group maintains that he died, but I am of the school that believe the fire that got out of hand spoiled his fun.

Conservation was becoming an issue in Turkey, prompted by the fate of the Caretta Caretta turtles at Dalyan and the monk seals near Bodrum. Situated between the two, the government declared Dereköy, miles of coastline and hills a class one conservation area. New building laws were issued and the much admired modern concrete box became a thing of the past. Instead of these wonders of cement, all new buildings were to be of the style of the picturesque wooden houses of old. Not far off the main highway and nestled in an attractive bay, we became a secondary stop-off for conservationists. Gentle souls could be seen wandering the hills with binoculars, getting over-excited when they saw what to us were everyday birds. These people treated the locals with respect and even attempted to understand the local ways.

Unfortunately there was another species of conservationist. Groups of angry young foreigners in the shortest of shorts, the briefest of vests and huge walking boots would congregate at the teahouse. If it wasn't the teahouse, it would be a café or the beach bar; they were rarely seen in areas where those clod-hopper boots could be considered an asset. Invariably they had a Turkish translator with them who spent the time he should have been lecturing the local men trying to explain why the young women had hairy legs and armpits. Some of the girls found a receptive audience and were pleased that so many village men would leave their tables and listen to their eco-fascist diatribe. Not one of these saviours of the world ever realised that it was the breasts, braless under the navvy's vest, which held the audience's rapt attention.

When they did occasionally make a foray into the countryside, they had no respect for private property as they stomped on plants, damaged fences and treated us all as imbeciles. At dusk one evening I found a group of them liberating Pog's boat, which they had filled with two crates of beer. They explained they were with the international something or other group and they were going down river to observe the otters. The mere mention of a respected conservation association appeared to give them the right to steal the dinghy. They only left, offended by my attitude, after I had tossed the beer into the river and chained the boat to the makeshift jetty. As they retreated up the track they hurled slogans at me; it would seem that I personally was the cause of the problems of our planet. These straggly flocks of aggressive young people over the next few years, along with the new building laws, made conservation a dirty word.

I still had no bridge over the stream from the gate. The water rushed between the large flat stepping stones and occasionally, when twigs and leaves blocked the channels, a dam would build up.

In early summer, barefoot in the water, I was clearing away the collected debris when I found a curious little packet. About 5 cm square and wrapped in plastic, it was sealed with masking tape. By the time I had finished my cleaning, I had three more of these mystery parcels.

Returning to the cottage, with the aid of a penknife I peeled the plastic covering off the first packet. Inside was a second layer of packaging made of cotton fabric of a pattern much favoured by the women of our village. Unpicking the stitches, I found a long narrow strip of paper inside with what looked like Arabic script covering one side of it.

As I sat looking at it, Baba Macit arrived to visit. One look at the horror on his face and I realised what they were. As he whispered, "*muska*", and moved his chair away from the packets on the table, I knew, although not understanding the word, that they were spells: black magic, harking back to beliefs pre-Islam. Somewhat shaken that these things could exist in our sleepy village and that someone had gone to such trouble to bring me harm, I was diverted by the arrival of Aydın and Solmaz.

Seeing the concern on the faces of my English-speaking friends, I said gaily, "Tell Baba not to worry; my western magic is stronger than this." Baba, being of the opinion that all imported things are superior, looked relieved. As I served tea he wanted to know the technical details of how to neutralise a spell. With Aydın translating and me making it up as I went along, between us we wove a convincing story.

First I must prepare the spells after dark and only by candle-light; next day before noon these must be placed around the property boundaries to cleanse the area. Getting carried away, I added that I would then chant a special incantation which would not only place permanent protection on me and mine, but would also rebound any evil, sending it back to plague the originator of the spells. I could see that Baba was itching to get up to the teahouse to repeat all to his cronies. By the time I walked to the village late afternoon the news was out. Songül at the grocery shop tied a blue bead on a leather thong around my wrist; the butcher dropped a glass boncuk into my basket and Hamza came across from his tailor's shop to give me a little book of Koranic verses. It was obvious they were worried, but their gifts would ward off evil.

That evening in the cottage I collected what odds and ends I felt would look authentic - scraps of ribbon, bay leaves, garlic - and made some tiny scrolls with mumbo-jumbo written on them. These I made into little posies, adding cotton padding from a cushion, with a large nail skewered into each garlic bulb as a final flourish.

Next morning I left the cottage with a tray of charms, a bowl of water and a candle. Baba Macit just happened to be examining the trees at the end of his orange grove, a position that gave him an uninterrupted view of our land. With a serious face, while pretending not to see him, I tied my first 'spell' to the barbed wire, dripped some candle wax onto the posy and then stood back. Lifting my arms in the air I sang the all- important incantation, "Baaaaa, Baaaaa, Bllaaaccck Sheep, Haave you any wooool?" Lowering my arms, I sprinkled water on the bunch of bits and pieces tied to the wire and moved on several metres to repeat the per-formance. I knew that before the day was out the whole village would know what I had done. I had no idea who had wished me ill will and soon forgot the whole thing, only occasionally being reminded by the disintegrating bunches tied to the fence.

A month later a monumental scandal erupted. Each day new details would emerge to be mulled over, embellished and savoured. The daughter of Haluk Bey had been found stark naked with an official from the Tax Department. The words 'stark naked' were whispered in horror. Şengül, mother of four, said that no man had every seen her naked and we all nodded in agreement. They had been meeting in a disused forestry hut and Haluk Bey's son-in-law, having become suspicious, followed his wife. The shame was all-encompassing; Haluk Bey no longer went to the teahouse and his wife was not leaving their home. The tax man had left the district with his love. The wronged husband's family spoke to no one related to Haluk Bey and the village was seething with recriminations and gossip.

After several weeks, although his wife had been seen in the garden, Haluk did not resume his visits to the teahouse. One day as I was walking to the village, I saw the family car coming towards me. He was driving with his wife beside him and his two sisters-in-law were in the back. When the women saw me, they suddenly ducked below window level and the driver appeared to be alone as he drove past me, looking rather puzzled by the women's behaviour.

I wondered what it was all about but realised a few weeks later when I called at Haluk Bey's house to ask for a root of mint. With much hand kissing and obsequious behaviour, the women of the family insisted in digging up their whole clump of mint while asking if there was anything else I wanted and offering to carry the clump to my cottage. To this day they dodge me if they can, all being firm believers in the potency of western magic.

That summer was filled with laughter and fun. Saus and Pog had invited just about everyone they knew to visit. I bought army tents and cots in Izmir and drew up a cooking roster. I am sitting here with a huge smile on my face as I remember those late breakfasts, the piles of washing in large plastic bowls which we trod as if we were crushing grapes for wine. The laughter and excursions, the faces changing as some left and others arrived, these young university students and sixth-formers were such delightful company; they must have been the cream of British youth. The villagers loved them, while I was dazzled by them. No discos, no drugs, no pre-packaged entertainment, and yet they all enjoyed the simple activities on offer. The cooks of the day would try to outdo previous menus and each evening we feasted. Lying on our backs under the trees, too full of food to move, we would gaze at the millions of stars and I would listen as they discussed their plans for tomorrow, their future careers or how they would change the world.

Our land and surrounding fields as well as the streams and river were dotted with pieces of ancient pottery. Soon we had a collection of shards and broken amphorae. One group dived in the river for days to salvage this treasure and we were all excited when Saus brought home a French archaeologist she had met at the bakery. Proudly we showed him our finds. He picked up one of the more treasured pieces, myopically squinted at it, and throwing it back on the table said, "It's only Roman."

Following the stunned silence as we all stood gaping at him, he explained that the Pharaohs sent ships to this bay to trade for frankincense. He showed us the frankincense trees which still grow wild here. Standing on a road where Alexander's armies marched was commonplace to him. To pass the 2,000 year old Carian tombs on the way to the highway was of no interest to him; he was looking for something older.

I looked at the villagers and wondered what a DNA test would tell us of their ancestors. Some of the traditions the women had embroidered into Islam hark back to Shaman rites, while much of Islam has been totally disregarded.

These people rarely bothered with national politics: whoever were in power made little difference in our forgotten corner of Turkey. Perhaps living surrounded by reminders of the past gave the locals a philosophical disposition. Alexander, Anthony, Cleopatra and, more recently, the Turkish President have visited this end of the bay. They've come, they've gone and life goes on; all beyond the village is transient.

Every day, one could find the young village boot-black at the teahouse perched on his little stool as he went about his business cleaning shoes. In the summer he sat under the mulberry tree and in the winter he had a special spot inside, next to the wood stove. He was a little slow mentally and prone to dramatic epileptic fits; the village men were very gentle with him and the owner of the teahouse would sometimes allow him to carry tea to the tables. Perhaps it was because his meagre takings supported himself and his widowed mother that the village men always had gleaming shoes. Although Dereköy was small, Hussein was never short of work. The first time I took several pairs of shoes to him for cleaning, his wooden crate of polishes and brushes had been replaced with a gleaming brass boot black box. He shyly showed me the little drawers, customer footrest and the glass jars with brass lids which held the liquid polishes. When I tried to give him a tip, he rummaged in a bag at his feet and presented me with a bunch of dried wild mountain sage.

Also ensconced at the teahouse was the village guard. A man who looked like an emaciated gnome, he wore the dirtiest, most frayed uniform I have ever seen. Apart from digging a grave when one was needed, I have never determined what else he did to earn his keep; I don't think he actually guarded anything except the teahouse.

Our *İmam* was responsible for two mosques, ours and the tiny one a mile away at the old port. Each day he endeavoured to be in two places at the same time. He would call the prayer at the village mosque, then, leaping onto his moped he would race to İskele to call the faithful there. As well as this daily challenge, he had to earn a living, as the government stipend was not a living wage. *İmams* all over Turkey have other employment and ours was in the tree-cutting business. In all weathers one would see him speeding between mosques or off to a job with his chainsaw strapped to the back of his bike. Across his chest he wore a gun holster in which he kept his walkie-talkie, which would crackle if he were needed back in the village.

One of our adventures that summer was to climb to the acropolis of the ancient city of Idyma. Only a few miles down the low road, Idyma is famed for absolutely nothing, although there is one rock tomb with a central column which archaeologists find mildly interesting. In the modern village at the foot of the steep hills one could see history in the modern dry stone walls and buildings: a lump of column here and a carved capital there, with numerous Roman roof tiles embedded in modern foundations. Of the ancient Carian city, only the rock tombs and the outline of the acropolis remain. Beyond the highest tomb the track ended and my intrepid offspring and their friends had to scramble through spiny scrub and clamber over rock falls. My enthusiasm evaporated at that last tomb and I opted to wait at the bottom. Sitting in the shade of a wild pomegranate, I watched the figures moving at a crawl towards the outcrop where I could see the crumbled ancient walls of the fortifi- cations. Soon I lost sight of them and, lying down for a moment, I closed my eyes. I dreamed of the past, of Alexander the Great's armies, of life in that city, now only remembered because of a tomb with a central column.

Voices woke me and I sat up to find four of our group standing in front of me in the gathering dusk. Their clothes were torn and they were scratched and bloody. The rest of the group were waiting for us further down the old road and, as I refuted any ideas that I had been asleep for hours, they regaled me with the afternoon's events. We should have had climbing gear, they announced chirpily as they explained how Saus had slipped over a steep drop and the only thing that saved her from certain death was a tree root she had managed to grab. While I had slept, my daughter had dangled over a cliff while Pog and Derek, the Camberwell art student, had risked life and limb to drag her back up. Meeting up with the rest of the party, I resisted throwing my arms around my offspring and feigned a non-chalance to keep intact my image of a cool mother.

The rostered cooks failed us that night and we ate cheese sandwiches downed with cheap wine as the tired, battered, conquering heroes waited their turn for the shower.

A few days before returning to school, Pog came home with a tiny wounded kitten. We couldn't begin to imagine how such a small scrap could have survived whatever had caused its injuries. One eye was missing, its tail had a dramatic kink, three paws looked like flippers and what little fur left clinging to his body was matted with blood, dirt and alive with fleas. We washed it gently in lukewarm water with a liberal dash of disinfectant. Immediately named Nelson, he lapped up a saucer of milk laced with brandy, then fell asleep or perhaps lapsed into a coma. Pog gently placed him in a box lined with an old tee-shirt and we both steeled ourselves to find a little dead body within hours.

Nelson was still with us next morning, bursting with energy, unbelievably ugly and filled to the brim with hate. He devoured his food and explored the garden, moving at speed with a peculiar drunken gait. Through the next few months he grew at an impressive rate, probably thanks to all the kitten dietary supplements Pog spent his pocket money on and posted from Gloucestershire. As Nelson grew, his fur came back in clumps of differing lengths and a vast range of colours. He was indescribably ugly and his malevolence blossomed to new heights. One had only to look at him for his unsightly fur to stand on end and, spitting, he would be poised to scratch the offender to death.

With the summer guests gone, I was left to the peace of the gentle rustle of the eucalyptus leaves, the murmur of the water splashing the stepping stones and the cat from hell.

CHAPTER 8.

AS AUTUMN ARRIVED and the days shortened, I wasn't sure that the cigar in the ashtray or the dressing gown on the bed would be enough to shore me emotionally through the winter. Solmaz and Aydın were off to Istanbul for an extended stay, and a long winter loomed.

Leaving the cottage in the less than capable hands of an alcoholic hippie who had wandered into the village in pursuit of a dream, I packed my airline bag and headed north. Nelson had been moved to the home of the village cat woman and, having paid for his bed and board, I left him baring his fangs at her motley collection of moggies. After a stay in Istanbul I moved on to Europe, joining the flotsam of travellers who circle the earth making brief alliances and drifting, killing time rather than face the *sans*-Selim dilemma. In a pension in Viareggio I whiled away weeks, on a yacht in Porto San Stephano, employed as a guard, I watched the unscrupulous staff of an Arab sheikh fritter his money. Back in Istanbul, on a whim I bought a rail ticket from Haydarpaşa to Victoria Station...just looking at those words on the ticket conjured up visions of adventures. Adventures there were. My first class sleeper didn't exist and most of the trip was spent sitting in the corridor. In Bulgaria the train filled up with drunken soldiers returning from leave; in Sofia where we changed trains I was sent in the wrong direction. Seconds before departure, a young man from a human rights organisation and I managed to throw ourselves into a carriage. We crouched all night amongst a mass of bodies outside the unusable (but well-used) lavatory. My very existence on earth riled this young Englishman and he ranted at me into the small hours of the morning. Wedged beside me was a handsome young Yugoslavian cigarette smuggler. He told me how Tito had made his country great. He spoke of how forward-looking the nation was. When we reached his destination he kissed my hand and said, "Come visit my country. Yugoslavia is modern; it is very western. We have chewing gum and jeans."

In London I was puzzled by friends' priorities and they in turn were bewildered by me. The memory of that gypsy winter is blurred and the only face sharply in focus is that of the young cigarette smuggler whose country was soon to plunge into chaos.

By spring I could think of nothing better than the cottage with a yachting magazine on the table. I arrived late at night, tired from the three-mile walk from the cross-roads, with my arms nearly dropping off from the weight of my baggage. The cottage was standing at the end of the overgrown track. The stepping stones had become a waterfall and fallen branches littered the clearing by the steps. As I unlocked and opened the door the stench hit me...for a moment I thought I would find a dead body. Hesitantly, I flicked the light switch and, miracle of miracles, I had electricity. The hippie was long gone, but not easily forgotten.

Beer cans littered the floor and were piled under the bed. The kitchen was beyond description. Every towel, sheet, cushion, every surface was filthy. My shoes stuck to the floor as I gazed at the smoke-stained walls, the cigarette burns on the table, the wall-to-wall filth and the indescribable state of the fridge and stove.

Suddenly I was tired no longer; I had to hurry...what would happen if Selim arrived to this? By morning the place was clean, with the bathroom full of bowls of soaking washing. The black mould was gone from the fridge and the stove was almost as good as new. Nothing was missing and the props were in place along with the slightly dog-eared boating magazine. I was on the first bus of the day to Muğla, where I bought a new mattress, pillows, sandpaper, paint and varnish. Osman strapped the mattress to the roof of the mini-bus and back in the village he and the passengers carried my purchases from the road to the cottage. With little sleep it took me five days of frenetic activity, but at last the walls were repainted, the table revarnished and everything was as it should be. On the night of the full moon the mattress, encouraged by piles of twigs and branches, made a wonderful bonfire. I was happy. I was home. The villagers gently welcomed me back, with a pat on the hand or a special smile. The *muhtar* steered me into his office and ordered tea. The owner of the largest boat at the quay, Captain Ahmet, greeted me as if he had spent the winter waiting for my return. Baba Macid had saved me a sack of oranges and the gifts of vegetables started again. The hedgerows were full of birds and the nightingales had become so tame they would not bother to fly to higher branches when I came out to sit on the doorstep in the evening. I no longer needed lists of chores to get through the days and the tension of waiting for Selim mellowed. People had stopped asking when he would be arriving and I no longer had to steel myself to answer their questions with a forced smile.

I avoided visiting Nurgül the cat lover for as long as possible, putting off the day of having to retrieve Nelson. Eventually feeling guilty over my delay, I made my way to her cottage; with luck the horrid animal may have been squashed by a speeding tractor. As I knocked on the gate, a head came out of an upstairs window and Nurgül started to wail. She begged me not to take Nelson; she loved him so much. As she opened the gate Nelson came stalking along the wall. He was now a huge snarling beast and, if it is possible, even more ugly. She crooned and babbled cattish noises at him as he behaved like a demented tiger. With a great show of reluctance I relinquished ownership of the horrid animal and managed to keep the lilt out of my step until I was safely round the corner.

In late May I went to Rhodes for the day. This was a trip most of the foreigners who lived in the Marmaris area did on a regular basis. I had never had the confidence or energy to face the paperwork involved in obtaining a residency stamp in my passport, so to renew one's three month visitor's visa, a trip out of the country for a day was enough. On the outward journey I recognised Captain Ahmet from the village, sitting in the passenger salon; as I lifted my arm to wave he gave a slight shake of his head and turned his back to me. As he disembarked in Rhodes I watched him disappear carrying a large suitcase. My five hours overseas were spent stocking up on the little luxuries not then available in south-western Turkey. As I dragged my heavy load of goodies towards the ferry terminal Captain Ahmet, without a hint of recognition, passed me with his large bag but minus the beautiful leather jacket he had been wearing that morning.

At the Turkish Customs hall while the local passengers were processed quickly, there was a long, slow-moving line of foreigners. The authorities were doing one of their occasional blitzes to apprehend those who work in tourism with no work permits. When my turn came, I left my bag on the floor as I handed over my passport. The customs officer standing next to the passport control desk asked me in Turkish to put my bag on the table. Pretending not to understand him, I made no move to comply, knowing this ruse often resulted in a dismissive wave of the officer's hand. He then in faultless English repeated his request and, defeated, I hauled my bag up for him to give it a cursory inspection. Unzipping it, he carefully removed each item and placed it on the table: the soy-sauce bottles, the fresh root ginger, Danish butter, French cheeses and peppermint creams all lined up with the oven cleaner and lesser treasures. Leaning forward, he very sternly asked me what all these goods were for. When I said they were for my husband, the most wonderful Turk in the world, he glowered and said, "Are you absolutely sure he is that wonderful?" Then with a smile he helped me repack the bag and I was on my way, a good hour after the ferry had docked. As I hauled my booty towards the bus stop, Captain Ahmet's orange VW Beetle swerved to a stop beside me. Greeting me as if we hadn't met for months, he tossed my luggage into the back seat and cheerily chatted as we drove to Dereköy. While he made no mention of Rhodes, I in turn ignored the lack of leather jacket and the now missing case.

Home with my shopping unpacked, I went into the garden to top up the water tank depleted by my long shower. It had been a very full day and sitting on the tree stump, I inhaled the scent of the eucalyptus as I waited for the overflow pipe to gurgle. I heard someone moving down the track towards me, but in the half light I couldn't see who it was. It was a man; he was carrying two suitcases. Stopping at the gate, he stood and looked at me. After two and a half years, Selim was home.

CHAPTER 9.

I WOULD LIKE to be able to write of a reunion worthy of a blockbuster movie, but the two suitcases and the row of stepping stones over the fast-running water were not props any film producer would include in such a scene.

Crossing the stream, I took one of the bags and we negotiated the stepping stones holding hands. At the steps looking at my packing crate table, Selim commented that he would make an outside table and chairs. I said I had just returned from Rhodes and he spoke of his flight from Istanbul being delayed. I made coffee while he put his bags in the bedroom and with our mugs we sat in silence, side by side, as the tears rolled down my face.

Next morning as we walked up to the village for bread, Baba Macit welcomed Selim home and assured him that a watchful eye had been kept on my every move. At the post office, Ekrem, who had spoken so often to my husband on the phone, did not know him and when recognition dawned, rushing to the telephone cabinet, he broadcast the news as he cranked the handle in a frenzy of excitement. Everyone had to shake our hands and congratulate us. So important was the event that Osman even abandoned his game of backgammon and Ahmet left a punter waiting in the taxi. Bustled into the *muhtar's* office by a group from the teahouse, Selim was brought up to date with every event of note that had occurred in the last two and a half years. Everyone claimed him as their long lost friend and had to talk to him. That afternoon we had a joyful celebration with Solmaz and Aydın: as Solmaz cried, Aydın pumped Selim's hand until I thought their arms would drop off.

The village had changed and there was much to show Selim. The summer people who had built a large villa close to the beach had in previous summers spent their evenings on the large upstairs balcony. The view of the sunset must have been glorious, but unfortunately they had not bought the closest plot of land to the beach. Now there was an equally splendid villa slap bang in front of them and we could see the family sitting on the balcony staring at a huge windowless concrete wall. Another very ornate new house had been built on reclaimed swamp and during the winter, subsidence had caused it to tilt drunkenly.

There was also the "Golden Spoon House," which attracted small groups who stood at the wall trying to peer in the windows. This huge luxurious villa was the property of a minor soap-opera star. She had met and had a whirlwind affair with an Arab oil minister. When the sheikh felt the need to move on, he had presented her with a diamond-encrusted 22-carat gold spoon as a farewell present. There is not much one can do with such a spoon, so the sale of this gift financed the construction of the actress's dream home. Nothing was too good for this lady's house and only the most expensive imported woods were acceptable. Stone for the foundations and garden wall was trucked in from a quarry 50 miles away. Each tile on the extensive balconies was hand painted in Ottoman tulip designs and even the grouting was imported from Germany.

The size of the spoon or the quality of the stones is not local knowledge, but whatever the dimensions, it was not large enough and the money ran out. Externally the house was complete, but the interior remained a shell. It stands behind a stone wall with tall elaborate carved wooden gates. There is no "For Sale" sign, so perhaps our actress is hoping to encounter another Arab bearing gifts.

A large hotel had been built on the inland slope of the village, as far as it is possible to be away from the sea. The people who had chosen this less than ideal site had made a fortune in Germany and were very aware that their wealth made them superior to the mere mortals of the village. They bought nothing locally and brought labourers and tradesmen from central Anatolia, deeming the locals unskilled. Not even a bag of nails was purchased at the local hardware store. The building completed, a grand opening was held with all the guests from out of town. Several village women were employed as cleaners, but as with the construction workers, the hotel staff were outsiders.

Within a day of the first load of German tourists being bussed in from Dalaman airport, the hotel began to have problems. Our village water supply was not able to cope with the extra load. The owners lowered themselves to visit the *muhtar*, suggesting he cut off the water to the rest of the village for a few hours each morning and evening. When they found Kemal Bey uncooperative, they sent a waiter to summon our local well-digging team, but they were too busy playing cards under the mulberry tree to take on a job. At great expense a drilling team arrived from Muğla and to everyone's amazement they couldn't find a drop of water.

`In a village where water never fails to gush, there was nothing but dry test holes. The small plot of land and cottage next to the hotel wall was the home of Ahmet the taxi driver; just meters from the dividing wall was Ahmet's artesian well with its unlimited supply of crystal-clear water. With the whole village advising Ahmet, the negotiations over the price of water dragged on long enough for two foreign tour companies to cancel their contracts. Once the water was flowing, the septic tanks filled rapidly and delicious stories of sewage flowing through the hotel kitchen kept the tea-house in glee-mode for weeks.

That first year, with cancelled contracts and the remaining companies sending their tourists to other towns, there were rarely more than a dozen guests. Prior to opening, the owners had briskly rebuffed other European tourist companies, preferring a German clientele. With the Germans gone, the second year they courted the French and British, but by then there was a second hotel, situated on the beach. The tour companies flocked to this hotel built and staffed by locals while the superior building on the wrong side of town eventually stood empty.

Late one afternoon as we were sitting in one of the beach cafés, we were joined by the English teacher who still had dreams of wooing Saus and, with marriage, gaining a British passport. This young man was the only truly horrid villager I had met. The son of illiterate parents who must have been well past the first flush of youth when blessed with a son, they had made massive sacrifices to keep him at school and later at university. They laboured hard on their few acres and the father would occasionally be seen riding his donkey to visit relatives in the next village. The teacher had distanced himself from his roots and told visitors to Dereköy he was from Marmaris. He would button-hole any English speaker to practice his fluency of the language and when he encountered a new word, he would write it phonetically in a little notebook to look up later. This day he had a problem and wanted our help. He had managed to have several long conversations with one of the English tourists and had written down one particularly tricky phrase. Handing us his notebook, written neatly were the words "bug are orv".

While the teacher's English is far from brilliant, I cannot criticise him. I've given up trying to communicate in anything but my basic English. Selim has forbidden me to utter my schoolgirl French - it makes him go pale and wince. The day I bought a tin of salmon, which turned out to be a tin of peas, I added two new words to my vocabulary. Beware of the tin with the picture of a mound of salmon decorated with a ring of peas!

I have an unbeatable knack of saying the wrong thing. For two years I said, "Excuse me" in Turkish when I meant "Good appetite", and worse, I said, "Good appetite" if I stood on someone's toes or knocked them down with my shopping trolley. My friend Jane asked the butcher for "chicken tits" instead of breasts for years.

The day I suggested to a Turkish gentleman during a business meeting that he obtain a circumcision (sünnet), when I actually meant an IOU (senet) was the day I decided to give up trying to be anything but uni-linguistic. It says a lot about the Turks' manners and tolerance that nobody ever corrected Jane or myself.

Some of the village women haven't realised I don't speak Turkish. They enjoy talking to me as I listen to their stories without interrupting. I nod occasionally and laugh or smile when they do. Sometimes I feel I have got the gist of the conversation but I am not that confident. At the grocer's shop this morning I was told about a child who threw a dog (köpek) out of an upstairs window. Then again, it could have been something about wholemeal flour (kepek), as Songül was arranging a shelf of baking ingredients as she spoke...

The humiliating thing is that so many Turks speak English and, after all the years I've lived here, I still have difficulty stringing a sentence together in Turkish. Fortunately the Turks are gracious and helpful when confronted by a foreigner who murders their language.

To be married to a Turk whose knowledge of my native tongue is far more comprehensive than my own can be galling. Until I got this magic machine with a spell-check I had to humble myself and ask him to proofread anything I wrote.

Selim's English is faultless, as I have said, but that summer it let him down. We had just bought four geese, which had promptly taken off down the river. They went inland and hid in the shrubs by Ibrahim's cottage. Selim rushed off to recapture them and on his return commented that the Englishwomen tourists at Ibrahim's were very odd. He said he'd asked them to help and they had rushed inside and locked the door.

Later in the day the tour rep visited. Did we know anything about a pervert lurking near the river? Apparently the two ladies in the quaint cottage, manophobes at the best of times, had been accosted. "What happened?" I asked. "Well, they're still hysterical, but I gather an evil-looking man ran down the garden path and said in perfect English, "Please, would you come into the bushes with me? I am on a wild goose chase."

Although we had met some of the English holiday makers, this was the first time we had met the young woman who was looking after the tourists who had come to Dereköy with an up-market London company. They had rented ten summerhouses and as Turkey was not yet a well-known tourist destination, her guests were on the whole rather adventurous types, not easily deterred by the village's lack of sophistication. The locals had directed some of her charges to us and we found ourselves involved in their queries or problems.

One afternoon Baba came down to tell us the English King's yacht was moored in the bay and the King was aboard. Curiosity aroused, on our way to the beach we learned that it wasn't an English king but Prince Charles aboard the Royal Yacht Britannia. Once at the jetty we could see a very modern Italian motor yacht, very un-Britannia like and it wasn't Prince Charles, but someone who knew him...or so it was said.

Later that week Selim was told that the head of the United Nations was coming that day to open a scout camp. We laughed and I took off to Marmaris for the day. That evening on arriving home I was met by a grinning husband. Perez de Cuellar had at 3 pm. officiated at the opening of the international scout camp a few miles further along the shore. Visiting the Turkish President at his summer house much further down the bay, the pair of them had popped in by helicopter to make a quick speech and cut the ribbon.

Soon Saus and Pog arrived with their friends, most of them already familiar with the kitchen and shopping rosters. Selim had decided that Pog needed a larger boat, and eventually a craft meeting every requirement was found. It was a local 7-metre fishing boat with solid cabin and a good diesel motor. A shopping list was drawn up and a day spent in Marmaris to buy ropes, canvas for a sun canopy, an ice-box, foam for a large mattress and a host of bits and pieces. The mattress made the cabin a wall-to-wall bed and there was a flurry of activity building shelves, stealing utensils from my kitchen and rushing up to the village for provisions.

That summer, every inch of shore for miles was explored and the young ones spent very little time ashore. The river water was ice cold, as it flowed from an underground lake fed by melted snow. One of the gang's favourite tricks was to pretend to any newcomer that the water was warm; as each of the group dived in, they had to surface with no sign that they would be turning blue in minutes. Chattering of teeth and shivering were not allowed as they encouraged the novice to jump from the anchored boat. Pog became a dedicated fisherman, and often the group would camp out for a night or two in some secluded bay.

Saus is not very fond of boating and she would often opt to stay home when extended outings were planned. One evening she and Selim were lying on rugs in the garden looking up at the sky crowded with stars. As they talked and set the world to rights, they were witness to what seemed to be hundreds of shooting stars. Much later we were told that it was the largest meteor shower in years.

One day Selim came home from the post office with a note from Nurgül the cat lover. The short letter announced that Nelson had become a daddy, as his wife had produced a litter of kittens. Nurgül felt so grateful that I had been kind enough to let her keep Nelson that she would like us to come and chose a replacement. I saw no need for a cat, and any kitten with Nelson's genes was definitely not welcome. In the short time since Selim arrived, we had acquired ducks and geese. My opinion was not even considered as the two animal lovers rushed off to visit the cattery. An hour later they were back with a small tabby bundle they had already named Finnegan. I was willing to tolerate this new addition to the family on the condition that he was an outdoor cat. For the next few weeks whenever I was safely out of the way, the cherished moggie became a house cat and several nasty messes were hastily cleaned up before I reappeared. They must have waited for one of my mellow moments, and eventually I accepted defeat. There was a large fishing weight on the end of a string which pulled the fly-wire door closed and this useless scrap of fur learned to swing the weight to knock on the closed door. Soon even I fell under his spell.

CHAPTER 10.

ONE MORNING AS we sat in the garden eating a late breakfast a visitor arrived at the gate. Announcing himself as an important businessman he asked to speak to the old woman. To the credit of my offspring and their friends nobody turned to me. But it was me this gentleman of note had come to visit. Handing me his card with a phone number written on the back, he ordered me in convoluted and atrocious English to immediately telephone the number. A most important lady in London wanted to speak to me and as the village outside line was down I must get to Muğla or Marmaris pronto. I am not a morning person, and two important people before I had finished my toast were a bit too much to mentally digest. As our illustrious guest bored Selim with a detailed account of his weighty position in society, I grappled with making a decision as to whether I would go fishing that morning. I had found a spot on the river much loved by trout. These fish occasionally escaped from the trout pool at the restaurant upstream. They grew fat and tasty in the river and were easy to catch using a thin strip of steak. My bait was a secret, as Pog would be horrified at such an unsporting activity and I had allowed him to think I used the flies he had crafted from bird feathers.

While Selim was ushering our VIP out the gate, Saus examined his card. He was hardly out of earshot when the merriment began. With just the smallest alteration of the letters of his name, he became Mr. Bumlick.

Pog and Selim had been planning a trip to Marmaris sometime that week to buy a part for the boat and swiftly it was decided that today was the day. I was chivvied off to shower and dress, as the group had decided Bummy was not going to be ignored and the old woman was to phone the important lady in London.

Once in Marmaris, the others headed off to the marina and I made my way to the line of telephones outside the post office. When I got through, a receptionist who had been expecting my call took my number and said Nita would ring me back. Nita turned out to be the owner of the English tour company whose guests had been coming to us for advice. The nice young rep had resigned, no longer able to cope with the problems of a village untrained to the needs of tourists. Guests returning to England had told her about Selim and I, and she had sent Bummy, her Turkish agent, to find us. "Would you take the rep's job?" she asked. The fact that I had never worked in tourism or even been on an organised holiday didn't seem to matter; she was obviously desperate. Nita said she would ring back in an hour and I went off to tell Pog and Selim of the conversation. To my surprise, Selim, with no hesitation, said I should take it. He figured that we would continue to be the tourism problem-solvers of the village and so we might as well be paid for our trouble. Nita was relieved and as the outgoing girl was leaving in four days, I was to learn everything from her before collecting my first group at the airport that Sunday. Nita's husband would be on the next incoming flight with her tourists and he would sort everything out.

Back in the village I located the rep, who seemed to have lost all interest in tourism. She handed me the paperwork, a map of where the houses were located and two rather snazzy uniforms. She instructed me to be at the top of our drive in uniform on Sunday at 10 a.m., and that was the end of my training programme.

The two sheds which had formerly been the terminal had been replaced by an impressive building. All too soon I found myself standing outside the doors of the arrival hall holding a smart clipboard with the company's logo on one side and a list of arriving guests on the other. Standing next to me was a small wiry Englishwoman with a board very much like mine. As we started to talk, it was soon obvious that here was my saviour. Margie with her Turkish husband had lived near Bodrum since the mid 70's and she had been working in tourism for years.

Welcome them with a smile, tick the names off the list, then send them to wait for you in some shady spot while you gather the rest of your group. Between smiles and list ticking she threw little titbits at me. Roll call on the bus...check all luggage is stowed...give them a short welcome speech...point out things of interest en route. When I asked what roadside sights would be considered interesting she gave me a despairing look and said, "Point out a field of sesame, tell them how it is harvested, then move into a spiel on Turkish cooking." Smile, tick. "Halva, sesame paste, you can go on forever." As we left she said she would meet me in the airport café next Sunday once I had shepherded my leavers through passport control. As we left the airport building, Bummy appeared and led the man I presumed to be Nita's husband to a gleaming Mercedes, calling to me they would see me in the village later.

Somehow, with more bravado than confidence, I got everyone plus baggage on board and located the driver asleep under a tree in the car park. An hour or so later, with everyone delivered to the correct villa, the bus dropped me at the top of our track where the Merc was already parked. The man who had come from London to sort everything out interrupted his conversation with Saus to hand me a sheaf of charts and lists along with an impressively large wad of money for expenses. He assured me I wouldn't have any problems, and that was the last I saw of Nita's husband, who left for a week's sailing with Bummy.

It wasn't long before I was feeling more confident and enjoying the guests, who in the main were not fazed by the erratic electricity or less than basic amenities of the village. The next time I spoke to Nita she said that her husband had enjoyed the days he had spent teaching me the ropes.

The following Sunday Margie gave me my first of many lessons on the tourism business. Up-market companies such as those we worked for had guests, never clients or even worse, punters. Have a few riveting lectures up your sleeve in case of emergencies, she advised. If a bus breaks down, move them into the shade and give them a talk on the history of Islam, or on women's place in society. "Alexander the Great tromped all round here...he's good for at least an hour." Always carry a first aid kit, I was advised; if you have got it, Sod's law, you won't need it. Many guests moved themselves up a notch or two socially on holiday, she told me. Keep your eyes open on the way back to the village and you will have sorted the nasties from the nice before you reach the villas. "Heaven help you," she said, "when you get a couple who hate each others guts...they can make your life hell and even ruin other people's holidays." Everything Margie told me proved correct over the next months. Why some people find it necessary to impress people they are never going to meet again, I cannot fathom, but it is a popular sport. "No, no, we didn't drive down this morning; we

-90-

stayed the night with friends in Virginia Waters, then left the Volvo at the airport." Little did the guest realise just how much I learned from such a statement.

Another interesting snippet was the importance of stress. Stress was very fashionable and proudly acknowledged. I would have thought that admitting that one's job was stressful was saying you hadn't got what it took to do the job...but no, stress showed how important the person was.

That second Sunday of my new career we had an elderly but sprightly couple who had brought all their food for the two-week holiday. "Even English eggs," the husband told me proudly. "We don't eat foreign muck." The other tourists quickly dubbed him Mr. Biggles, as he spoke in one of those 1950's BBC accents as he talked about fuzzy-wuzzies and infidels. That fortnight it became a game, played with dedication by every English speaking person in town, to avoid Mr. Biggles. The Saturday after they arrived he cornered me to ask what time mass was held. His wife always went to early mass on Sunday; in fact she hadn't missed a service in twenty years. When I explained that Izmir had a Catholic church, but it was a five hour drive, he announced to the teahouse and bus queue that I was a per-verted liar whom he was going to report to the travel company as well as the British Tourist Board.

Within the month we had a teenager run away from home and land up at our place. This girl had a huge argu-ment with her father and walked out vowing never to return. Unfortunately, they were into their second day of a holiday in a Turkish village, not home in Chiswick. Leaving her with Pog and friends, I rushed off to smooth out the situation. As I entered the gate the father came to the door, and the man who had been so charming the day before shouted, "I'm not having that little bitch back here; she's your problem, not mine." A more experienced rep would have handled it differently, but I meekly left and installed her in one of the tents in our garden.

This child had just finished her A Levels and was soon to start her first year at university. Having been with us several days, she confided to Pog that she had decided to discard her virginity before she embarked on her tertiary education. He had been chosen to perform the deed. A huddled family conference was convened in the kitchen and although there was nothing in the Tour Rep Manual to cover the situation, we agreed that it probably would have been included in the rules laid out in the sexual conduct section, if the author had envisaged such a state of affairs. After waking one night to find the girl sitting on his bed, stroking his thigh, Pog took to sleeping in the salon with the door locked. Derek, hairy and unkempt, generously offered his services, but it had to be Pog. On departure day she sat at the front of the bus while her family sat at the back. Her airline ticket was passed hand to hand up to me and when I bade her farewell at passport control, she and her family walked through without speaking. That was the last we ever saw or heard of them. It was just one of those little stories in life which is missing the final chapter.

Very early in my new career it became obvious that we needed organised tours for the guests. Osman and his two brothers who also had mini-buses became our fleet and I began to burn the midnight oil as I swotted up on the history of nearby ancient sites. The Dalyan tour fast became a favourite and was so popular that one week, with extra mini-buses from other villages, we formed a convoy of seven village vehicles. At various spots on the road we would stop and I would give a little talk on the stork colony or a field of cotton. One week when we were off on the marathon trek to Ephesus, I must have dozed off. I was jolted awake to find the lead bus stopped on the roadside. Osman was prodding me and repeatedly hissing, "Rowmen blidge". Gathering my thoughts, I was able to leap off the bus and deliver my usual speech about the ancient Roman bridge beside the modern road.

Although Osman's clan joined in this new venture with enthusiasm, it took two tourist seasons to sort out the wrinkles. They had no conception of running to a timetable and were bewildered by my demands for punctuality, convinced I was mentally ill when I had the occasional temper tantrum. Arriving back at the buses hot and tired after a day of shepherding my little flock, it was not uncommon to find no drivers, and a search of the local teahouses had to be instigated. Once there weren't even driverless buses...nothing. I had to lie through my teeth and send everyone off for ice-creams while I started a bus search. One week I threatened to defect and use Marmaris buses if the lot of them were not on time for the Ephesus trip next day. Coming home at midnight, we found the lane to the house blocked by three buses; peering in the windows we could see the drivers asleep in the back seats. Rather than risk my wrath, the brothers had decided to sleep on site ready for the 7 a.m. start. Next morning I had to explain to the group why our drivers were unshaven and sporting wrinkled shirts and trousers.

Sometimes the brothers would indulge in a little extra commerce on the side, and I would ignore the crates of vegetables heaped on the roof racks. Occasionally in the name of commerce, Osman would suggest we do the tiniest of detours and I would give him a hard time pretending I had no idea why we should visit an unscheduled village.

The tourists who had made a leap in their social status between Heathrow and Dalaman were, without fail, patronising toward me and mine. On one outing, Pog and his friend Hischam had joined us. Hischam, with Sudanese ancestry, was as dark as red-headed Pog was fair; both of them six foot four and handsome, they made a startling pair. One of our least liked guests decided to have a condescending conversation with them. After asking Pog if he had gone to school in England, she asked what school. Having recognised the name, she obviously found it difficult to believe that a rep's son could go to a school she found socially acceptable. Turning to Hischam, she asked the same question and was told Eton. The whole bus smirked as she sat trying to assimilate this knowledge; her friendliness for the rest of her stay was a joy to behold.

One ghastly man from the Channel Islands decided that Selim should speak French, and gave him a list of ten words to learn. He made Selim repeat each word after him, and Selim complied, carefully imitating his teacher's atrocious accent. At the end of his holiday as the bus was leaving for the airport, Monsieur Crapaud, with much ado and pomposity, gathered those departing around him and my husband. He instructed his student to repeat the words and told him that he should learn a word a day and soon he would speak basic French. The few people on the bus who knew Selim's first language was French fast spread the word and I had to beg them not to tell our Channel Island guest.

In those early days the boats at Dalyan which ferried tourists to the sites were not as strictly controlled as in later years. If a boat was said to be big enough for 30 passengers I would only put 15 people on it, and my guests would sit comfortably with room to sprawl while other groups would pass us on boats packed to the gunnels. When we were on a multi-boat excursion, Saus or Pog would accompany me to be the guide on the second boat. Late one afternoon as our boats were heading back to Dalyan, those of us in my boat were lolled on the seats, relaxed and tired after a full day. On a straight stretch halfway up the river our second boat captain started to play games and it appeared as if Pog's lot were ready for a race. Everyone was waving at us and pointing, but my son, looking panic-stricken, was shouting at me. I couldn't make out a word and was convinced someone had had a heart attack. As the boat came level with us, the boatman manoeuvred alongside and Pog leapt five feet to land on our towel-strewn deck. As he landed he almost flew aft to the tiller and it was only then that we realised we were chugging along with no one at the helm. While we had been frolicking on the white sands of Dalyan beach, our captain had been quenching his thirst with liberal swigs of raki, the potent Turkish national alcoholic beverage. At the beginning of the straight stretch of water he, even more relaxed than his passengers, had toppled over the stern. The most amazing thing was that nobody got angry or upset, but just treated the incident as a highlight of the tour.

CHAPTER 11.

WITH OUR LAST guests gone, we prepared for our first winter together in Dereköy. Selim had added many little touches that made the cottage more comfortable. Shelves in the kitchen, bedside tables and a bookcase in the salon had been made, as well as a stout bridge over the stream. The sky was filled with storks migrating to warmer climes and the camel man did a thriving trade in delivering fodder for winter feed. We spent several days cleaning dead leaves from the roof and replacing tiles broken by the small eucalyptus branches which had fallen during the summer. The summer tents and cots were stowed in the little workshop Selim had built on the back of the house. The hammocks were taken down from the trees and the woodpile was once again replenished.

We didn't notice the broken shutter or anything untoward when we came home from a day out in Marmaris. It was only when Selim went to turn on the radio and it wasn't there that, taking stock, we realised we had been robbed. As well as the radio, our camera and binoculars had gone. A search added deck-shoes, clothes, various trinkets and two packets of biscuits to the list. From my bedside table along with the clock, a Christmas-cracker type of necklace had gone. It had been a present from a Saudi sheikh and although I vaguely knew it was valuable, the loss of our little digital radio was far more upsetting.

The *jandarma* arrived and examined the scene of the crime, but held little hope that anyone would be apprehended. At the time we were babysitting a large German shepherd dog, which we pretended was very fierce. The corporal was surprised that the thief had been brave enough to enter the property. Selim reconciled himself to the loss and had bars fitted to the window while I fumed.

A few days later we had a phone call from the local gendarme chief. The thief had been apprehended in Marmaris; he had taken my garish necklace to a Marmaris jeweller saying it was his mother's and she wanted to sell it. With one look at the cluster of diamonds and sapphires, the jeweller decided that this was not the property of a village woman. He told the youth that he wasn't interested but he had a friend who was, and promptly telephoned the police. Although caught in Marmaris, he had to be brought to Dereköy to be charged. As there was no free vehicle at the gendarme station, Selim was asked to drive two jandarmas to Marmaris and bring them and our thief back. At the Marmaris Police Station the evil felon turned out to be a thin, pale sixteen year old sitting with bent head as a sergeant gave him a fatherly lecture. The jandarmas and Selim signed forms for the delivery of the hand-cuffed lad who was marched between the two gun-toting *jandarmas* to our car.

Next morning the boy was brought to our house to show how he had gained entry, and to be persuaded to confess to where he had stashed our belongings. His memory was hazy until the corporal suggested he might like to go down the garden with me, where I may be able to help him recollect where our property had been hidden. As I had been making hissing noises and an occasional snarl, this suggestion immediately cleared his thoughts and he was able to lead us to a pile of hay in a nearby field. There, hidden under a sack, was my overnight bag, which we hadn't realised had been stolen. Inside was everything we had noticed missing plus several items we weren't aware had disappeared.

All my liberal attitudes flew out the window when I watched the boy re-enact his forced entry into the cottage. As he stood beside my bed with his grubby feet and demonstrated how he had rummaged through my bedside drawers, my feelings swerved to a stance slightly to the right of Genghis Khan, and tossing the wretch in boiling oil would have been too lenient as far as I was concerned. I screamed at him in English and he was happy to be carted off by the *jandarmas* to the safety of a cell. Never before or since have I had four men and two guns crowded into my extremely small bedroom.

The senior gendarme knew the youth's family in the next village well, and had warned the boy earlier that he would land in trouble if he didn't change his ways. Now, of course, it was too late, and he had shamed his parents. His father could not face his cronies in the teahouse and his mother was overcome with grief. To them this was a permanent stain on the family which could never be erased or forgotten.

We were notified that the court, based 25 miles away, would convene at our home a week later. This I found amazing, but was told it was to ensure that the judge could clearly assess the situation. On the awaited morning Selim arranged chairs at our garden table and I polished the tea glasses. At 2 p.m. a dolmuş and two cars arrived at the top of the track. The judge, the court usher, the driver and two men whose roles were undefined made their way to the gate with the lady stenographer staggering along behind them with her arms wrapped round her huge typewriter. The cars belonged to two of our village elders, who had been notified by the court that they were to attend. A few minutes later, the boy in handcuffs was escorted down the track by two new *jandarmas*, with the two from the trip to Marmaris forming a rear guard. I had expected his parents to attend, but there was no sign of a representative from the family. At this stage I had to do a quick sprint up Baba's orchard to borrow more chairs and tea glasses.

When everyone had sorted themselves according to rank around the table, the proceedings commenced as tea was passed around. Once again, the boy had to demonstrate how he had smashed the shutter with a stone, but fortunately the judge stopped short of taking the court into the bedroom. He was very gentle with the boy as he asked questions, and I began to feel that it was all our fault for putting our shuttered window in front of the stone. Asked why he had not been afraid of the dog, the boy shattered our illusions by answering that everybody knew the dog was stupid.

The judge then asked for Selim's full name and date of birth. The stenographer was head down belting the keys of her machine with gusto, the gendarme were stood to attention and the boy, who had shown no sign of remorse a week earlier, looked as if he expected to be hung by the neck until dead. When the judge asked for my date of birth, the two village elders who had been lounging in their chairs suddenly perked up. There has always been curiosity as to my age in the village and I have always thwarted attempts to find out. I told the judge that Englishwomen never disclose their ages. He looked at me sternly, then at the eager elders. Passing me a piece of paper he asked me to write it down; he then gave it to the stenographer saying, "This information is confidential to the court records." With this statement, the two locals lost interest again and sat in bored silence.

The fact that a forced entry had been made and the ugly necklace valued at a large figure by the Marmaris jeweller weighed heavily against the boy. That he was underage and it was his first conviction lessened his sentence. He was given six months and would have to serve three. We were asked if we wanted to press further charges but Selim said no, and as there was no chance of beheading him or the boiling oil option, I lost interest and pretended to be liberal, understanding and gracious. When we were asked if we wanted to say anything, Selim gave the lad a gentle talk about learning his lesson from this escapade.

I have never seen him since; perhaps following his incarceration the family sent him to relatives in some remote corner of Anatolia. My anger has abated, but years later those poor parents, pillars of the community, continue to be shamed by their son's crime.

CHAPTER 12.

MY HUSBAND HAD spoken little in the past of his family or his childhood in his grandparents' house in Lebanon, but that winter as we sat in the tiny salon, often with only a candle for light, he began to reminisce.

Selim's grandmother was the daughter of the eldest son of Sultan Abdul Hamid II. Princess Emine was brought up in the sheltered environment of her father's palace. For the first twenty-one years of her life her grandfather was the ruling Sultan and as his oldest grandchild, hers was a very privileged position. Her father, HIH Prince Mehmet Selim, was a man of such modern ideas he was often at odds with the Sultan. His daughter's education was comprehensive, including Turkish, French, Farsi and mathematics.

When the time came for the Princess to marry, her father told his daughter that he thought arranged marriages were old-fashioned and presented her with the photographs of three eligible bachelors. "Here you are" he said, "You may choose your own husband."

One of the three was a startlingly handsome young man who was Turkey's first qualified mining engineer, having graduated from the Lycée Louis le Grand, the École Polytechnique de Paris and the École des Mines. As well as being incredibly handsome, Ali Kenan was the son of a national hero and perhaps these considerations had something to do with his photo being her first choice. But unknown to her father, the bride-to-be was also very modern. Her mother had died seven years earlier and her lady-in-waiting Missel Hanim had become her closest companion and confidant. In great secrecy, Missel was instructed to locate and meet the manservant of the chosen young man. I can see in my mind's eye these two women seated on Grandmother's huge canopied four-poster while they plotted and schemed this daring excursion. Following a week of intrigue, it was arranged that the Princess and Ali Kenan would meet by a newspaper kiosk in the Gülhane Park. In the manner of the French romantic novellas of the time, so loved by Princess Emine, Ali Kenan was to carry a certain newspaper under his left arm while she would be carrying a violet parasol. The fact that she was arriving in a royal coach and would immediately be recognised was a detail that seems to have escaped our young lady.

On the appointed day the young couple, complete with parasol and newspaper, met and a short, hurried conversation ensued. What they spoke of I do not know, but whatever the conversation was, it removed any doubts from Grandmother's mind; safely back at the palace, she informed HIH Prince Mehmet Selim of her choice.

Damat Ali Kenan later said that he fell in love in Gülhane Park that day. Through thick and thin (and believe me, there was a lot of thin), this couple adored each other until Damat Ali Kenan's death over fifty years later.

Following the acceptance of Ali Kenan as the chosen bride-groom, it was now his duty to present a ram to the family of the bride. He and his brother combed Istanbul for the healthiest, most perfect ram they could find and the two brothers had much fun as they inspected flock after flock. Eventually the ram was found and fed sweet marjoram and thyme to sweeten its breath; it was shampooed and brushed, and its horns and hooves repeatedly polished with rose oil. On the day of delivery Grandfather and his brother Seyfullah gave the animal a last inspection. Uncle Seyfullah was the one who realised that a terrible mistake had been made. The so carefully selected ram was not perfect at all; it had a patch of black fur encircling one eye, but not the other. Perhaps Uncle Seyfullah was teasing, but in panic Ali Kenan, with brush and India ink, painted a matching patch around the other eye. Presumably all went well because wedding plans were commenced.

Princess Emine was to have two wedding dresses, one from Paris and one of oriental style. In the nearly life-size photo-graph in the Istanbul Aunt's salon of the bride in her oriental dress, the style looks extremely Parisian to me, and in the painting belonging to the Beirut Aunt, the Parisian dress has a definite oriental flavour.

Her Grandfather, having been deposed and exiled two years earlier, managed to send a wedding gift of a box of fruit from Salonica. It was said that the melons were full of glittering gems, but if so, Emine never felt the need to clarify the story. The wedding was held at the Yildiz Palace and the photographs show a Clark Gable look-alike groom and a very serious young bride with large solemn eyes.

In 1923 the Sultanate was officially annulled and in late April of 1924 the leaders of the new Republic announced their decision to exile the royal family. They were given little time to prepare, and as they packed, Grandfather was called to the headquarters of the new government. He was offered the position of Head of the Ministry of Mining and a whopping salary. Many of the husbands of Princesses stayed to be part of the new regime, while their wives and children were exiled. Ali Kenan, who would not desert his wife and children, was treated to a stern lecture by the new leader. He was not convinced; and so, stripped of their Turkish citizenship, he left with his wife and three children along with over 120 family members and their retainers. Prince Mehmet Selim had decided to go to Lebanon with his son, while Princess Emine with her husband and children left aboard the Orient Express bound for Paris.

Throughout that winter I built up a picture of the lives, adventures and tragedies experienced by the family in exile and began to understand a little better the Istanbul Aunt who lived in a world totally removed from the realities of today.

While I was alone I had not paid much attention to cooking, but now the Turk was home, a boiled egg and toast for dinner was no longer acceptable.

All my favourite recipes are from pre-1970 cookery books - for reasons immediately understood by anyone living a twelve-hour drive from the nearest cosmopolitan city. Older recipes will require something known quite simply as "flour". That means the stuff I can buy at Mehmet's corner shop. They don't demand "strong flour", "bran-enriched flour", rye flour or gluten-free flour. No, flour was flour in those days - and still is, so far from Istanbul.

Have you any idea of how many mustards those modern cookery people think I can lay my hands on? Then they throw in things like double cream, Grand Marnier, preserved ginger, or ingredients totally unheard of in this part of the world, such as crème fraiche or balsamic vinegar.

Here we still have things called "seasons" - something out of history to most people, I imagine. I can only buy carrots at the time of the year when carrots grow locally. We go through a month or two of geriatric potatoes before the new crop appears.

Even with the good old basic recipes there is a lot of compromise. One night I decided to make Beef Wellington, and when the finished product was put on the table it looked magnificent. Selim commented that it was delicious and asked its name. When I told him, he put his knife and fork down and grinned.

"Doesn't Beef Wellington have mushrooms?" he asked.

"Yes, but I couldn't find any, so I used spinach."

"Pate?"

"There were no chicken livers in the market so I used mashed potato with a dash of soya sauce."

"Pastry?"

"I was running late so I used Turkish filo."

"Ah," he said. "Well, it is definitely beef, but I'm not sure about the Wellington."

After this example of compromise overkill, I began to make an effort to produce Turkish food. I had chosen *İmam Bayıldı*, (an eggplant dish) as my first foray into the realms of a new world of cuisine, having the wit to know that one cooks what is in season in the region. Armed with my list, I headed off to catch the dolmuş to Muğla market, a market where it seems to me every item of produce available in the whole of Turkey has been gathered, leaving the rest of the country and perhaps the Middle East bereft of food. Each visit I wonder anew as I gaze at the vast mountains of fruit and vegetables which stretch for acres in a profusion of colours.

Now the first step is vitally important: it is not just a matter of grabbing six eggplants, paying for them and moving on to the next item on the list. First I had to examine and choose the eggplant, feigning confidence as I watched what the other buyers were selecting. Having never actually handled an eggplant before was not really a problem; I just noted which were being rejected by the Turkish house-wives and learned what isn't acceptable. I learned quickly to shop at a small stall and ingratiate myself with the owner. If the stallholder has trouble finding a plastic bag, I take a pile of bags with me the next time I am shopping. I always have plenty of small change, and behave as I imagine the perfect customer would. Within a few weeks I was on the privileged regular customer list and the stall-holders went out of their way to understand my creative Turkish. Soon I reached the heady position of being supplied from the fresh sack, not yet on view to the mere hoi polloi. After a time I felt I was an extension of the family and I had many happy conversations larded with sign language, the produce becoming a secondary consideration on my visits to the market these days.

Having assembled the ingredients, it is simple to follow the recipe, although I would suggest a stiff drink or a few Valium before trying to stuff vine or cabbage leaves.

The first time I served *İmam Bayıldı* to a Turkish family, the wife praised my endeavours but gently suggested that a little less onion and a little more parsley would make it perfect. Following her advice, it was suggested by another lady on my second attempt to add another couple of onions and cut down on the parsley.

This problem has been solved and there is now a map of Turkey inside the cover of my local recipe book. I ascertain exactly what part of Turkey our guests are from; if it's Istanbul, I find a town on the map a good distance from their home base. Then as the dish is served, I say, "This is a recipe a lady from Zonguldak gave me." This ploy has eliminated any hint of advice, and once I was even asked for the ingredient quantities. This ruse has also done my knowledge of Turkish geography a world of good.

CHAPTER 13.

BY MID-SPRING WE had added a flock of bantams to the menagerie of ducks and geese. The bantam rooster was a beautiful creature with the most evil temper; I cannot remember why we gave him the innocuous name of Fred: he should have been dubbed Lucifer. The only person he would tolerate was Selim, who had rescued him and his harem from imprisonment in a dirty cramped cage. Fred would spring into the air with talons bared whenever I got too close; as I walked down a path, suddenly there would be a hair-raising squawk and a bundle of feathers would hurl towards my ankles. I recognised him as an enemy and rarely gave him the opportunity to slash my ankles. Guests had to be warned: Fréd preened and strutted for an audience and as the gullible admired him, he would be sidling into position to attack. The ducks were a wonderful asset; spending their days bottom up in the water, they took over the job of cleaning the streams and river. The geese were less welcome; their noisy and bad-tempered nature may have been tolerable but they excreted, at high velocity, vile green muck over just about every square inch of the land. When they attacked and killed our first brood of ducklings, Selim gave them to the owner of a restaurant on the river where they are fed and appreciated by diners who, because of the steep riverbank, are not treated to their less attractive habits

That year a second English tour company moved into the village and Selim took the job of hosting the guests. We had great fun working in competition, and would hurl insults at each other from passing buses. Once the tourists twigged we were husband and wife, they joined in the sport. Selim's job did not involve him going to the airport, so with luck sometimes I would meet some of his group before they headed off to the village. I would warn them that their rep was a Turkish villager, with very little English, while he would tell mine I had only been in Turkey two weeks and knew nothing.

I enjoyed the weekly trip to the airport, especially the half an hour or so between saying farewell to one group and waiting for the next. The reps for the different companies would meet in the airport café and I met other British women who had chosen to live in Turkey. Margie had been a high-powered executive in the UK before choosing to live in a Turkish village. Pat was a retired archaeologist and Jane had been something important in one of the top London hotels. I have yet to meet anyone who knows more about tourism than Jane. She later took over my job so I could concentrate on the tours. Nita got the best bargain of her life when Jane took her Turkish operation in hand.

When the new arrivals had reached the baggage hall, we would line up with our boards and welcome smiles. One week two beautiful young men in full make-up came hand in hand through the arrivals door. We all held our breath as we waited to see which of us they would approach. Fortunately it was Pat, who was based in Bodrum where such a pair wouldn't cause a ripple. I was almost dizzy with relief...Dereköy was not yet ready for such guests. Another week a group arrived with three windsurfers...they were mine. The family had not thought they may cause a transport problem and they were a little cross when Osman tied the boards to the roof of the bus. Throughout their holiday they did little to endear themselves to the other guests, or me, and unfortunately they enjoyed themselves so much they came back for several years running.

Because the numbers both companies sent to Dereköy were small, we combined our tours, and early in the season I had sixteen tourists on an Ephesus trip. Previously there had never been enough money to cover costs as well as the luxury of a guide but, with the numbers suddenly reaching crowd proportions, this was going to be my first professionally guided tour.

When we reached the gate of the city I gave the group ten minutes to have a drink and told them grandly I would find our guide, saying it as if it was merely routine. I knew nothing about the process of hiring a guide, but as a clutch of them always sat on a bench just inside the gate I envisaged no problems.

On reaching the seat under the trees, I found that there wasn't a guide in sight. There was a thin, frail man hunched on the bench. Stretched out in front of him were his crooked, twisted legs and propped against the curb were two metal walking sticks. As I turned away he called out in English, "Can I help you?" "Thank you, but I am looking for a guide." "I am a guide," he replied.

What could I do? I could hardly say that I had changed my mind, but it was obvious that I was heading for a disaster of horrible proportions. We negotiated a price, exchanged names and after he had asked me what kind of people my guests were, I headed back to find the group.

Meeting my flock at the admission kiosk and putting on a brave front, I told them that our guide was waiting for us. Then I added that I had not told them earlier, but Naci was severely handicapped, so it meant that we got a nice unhurried tour. This, I felt, was better than saying that we'd be lucky to be through by midnight.

Naci took us into the shade, sat us all on a fallen column and proceeded to give us a most comprehensive, concise history lesson. So far, so good. In fact so far, brilliant; as long as we didn't have to move, all looked fine. But the moment had to come and when it did, Naci, wielding his metal sticks, did a sort of wild pirouette and told us to follow him. He took off like a bullet; legs in all directions, he moved at an unbelievably brisk pace towards the first site he wanted to show us. Some of my group, who fifteen minutes earlier had been elderly verging on infirm suddenly became vigorous and even athletic.

Having read everything I could lay my hands on about Ephesus, I wasn't expecting to learn much but Naci showed me a city I had never seen. He brought it alive and his knowledge was awesome. When he went down the theatre steps at about fifty miles an hour I had to shut my eyes and several times I had to slink off to take a rest. Ephesus was his passion; he knew all the archaeologists by name and there was not a thing about the city he did not know. In the winter he travelled to Europe and America, where he had a permanent invitation to give lectures.

Only much later did I learn that he was on the bench that day because a group had cancelled. He doesn't have to tout for work; he has his regular tours and is booked for every day of the season. Fortunately he liked my group because they asked intelligent questions, and fitted us into his busy regular schedule.

On the way home after a wonderful day, one of the ladies commented that I had a wry sense of humour, talking of a leisurely tour with Naci. She said she had got quite a shock when he took off at such a pace. Shock...she didn't know the meaning of the word!

For our trips to Cleopatra Island we hired one of the larger boats moored down by the jetty. Captain Ahmet was never the stereotype of a village fisherman. Dapper and courtly, apart from that earlier Rhodes outing he had always made me feel I was the one person he wanted to meet. He can be seen on balmy summer nights, wining and dining tourist ladies in restaurants a seemly distance from our village. Bülent his helper is a descendent of the cotton plantation slaves; fat and dark-skinned, he could always be relied upon to be sporting the most amazing hair cut. A scarlet Mohican, purple stripes, or plaited extensions half way down his back, he added a touch of the exotic to every boat trip.

In winter the Captain and his sidekick fish the bay, but in the summer his boat caters to the tourist needs of sun, sand and a drop of culture. He has found from years of experience that most punters like half an hour of ancient site but definitely not more. He is known locally as Tak-Tak Ahmet - he earned his nickname in the Seventies when he was seen, after severe provocation, to shoot in the general direction of two customs officers. At that time foreign spirits and cigarettes were always readily available around here, while not easily found in most parts of Turkey. It is said that he used to find the fishing good near the Greek island of Cos, and indeed he always returned with a fine catch of bream.

That summer we were cruising the bay with a party of tourists when Captain Ahmet spied a large fishing trawler with its nets spread across the deep inlet. Not only was netting illegal, but far worse, it was not a local boat. Quietly issuing orders, my hero steered into the nets. Badly tangled, our steering malfunctioned and we went round and round in circles.

The fish thieves shouted and gesticulated while our captain apologised as his boat continued to swathe itself in their nets. With the steering partly corrected, we jerked first to port, then to starboard, ensnaring more and more net, before returning to our uncontrollable circling. Ahmet appeared to have turned into an incompetent idiot, and only once I'd assured the bewildered tourists that in reality he was anything but a fool did they join in with shouts and wild waving.

Eventually, tired of his game or perhaps of hearing his mother's origins maligned, our captain stopped his motor and Bülent was ordered over the side to cut our propeller and rudder free. Anchored in the bay, we watched the trawler as it headed off to Bodrum, and Bülent, in the name of conservation, passed the hat round. I knew no conservation group would see the donations, but I felt they had earned a tip for the unscheduled entertainment.

At the end of the tourist season I heard that that my two seafaring friends were in prison for a bit of a rest. But I was reassured by Tak-Tak's son that his father was quite comfortable and would be home for the *bayram* holiday.

Bülent usually spends a few days in custody each summer, due to his habit of baring his male particulars to chosen lady tourists. More often than not, this adds a saucy note to the honoured one's holiday. But occasionally Bülent's one-man show is not appreciated, so the outraged lady is placated by our captain bellowing and beating his miscreant around the head. Our *jandarma* are always outraged as they haul him off for a spell under lock and key until the distressed visitor's holiday is over.

This time it seemed things were more serious. Ahmet was accused of dynamiting fish. His home and boat were searched but no evidence was found. This, of course, should have been the end of the matter, as laws have always been somewhat elastic in this area. Unfortunately, the new-broom gendarme chief was a bit gung-ho. Bülent's hut was searched and, alas, not only were bomb ingredients found, but 98 foreign T-shirts and 67 pairs of sunglasses. Bülent claimed that he had been framed by the Mafia, but to no avail.

To deter all the rest of us from evil acts, our captain's mate has been made an example of. Bülent wasn't to be seen until the next summer. But locals told me his hut was very draughty in the winter, so all in all he was quite happy.

The Cleopatra Island trip was one of my favourites. We didn't board the boat until 9.30, so I wasn't crawling out of bed at the crack of dawn. Captain Ahmet took over my role of host and I was able to sit back and enjoy the hour's ride to the island. The sea was always that unbelievable blue one sees in brochures, and the tall mountains on each shore made an impressive backdrop. Just occasionally we would see the family of dolphins that live in the bay and Bülent could be relied on to point out the vestiges of the many ancient forts which dotted the shore. In antiquity this had been a busy route, with ships from Egypt and other distant shores arriving to load with wood, cotton, wine and the frankincense from the Liquid Amber Orientalis trees which grow wild in the area. Looking back towards Dereköy, one could see the Genoese fort behind the village and on the other side of the bay was its counterpart guarding the end of the inlet.

At the island I would take the group to see the beach famed for its distinctive sand. Legend has it that Mark Antony had it shipped from Egypt to make a perfect beach for his love. The couple is known by historians to have been in the area, but modern marine biologists maintain that the perfectly spherical grains of sand are fossilised plankton, which evolved locally. There is no other beach in the area where this sand can be found, so I prefer to believe local folklore. Behind the beach are the remains of the small city of Cedraea. Few of the tour guides bother to show their groups this ancient site and there was always something special about being the only ones scrambling over the rough track amongst the twisted olive trees. There is a miniature Roman theatre where, away from the noise of the beach, I would feel each time as if I had just discovered it. We would sit in the shade of a tree in the upper tiers of seats and I would relate the local history. We would scramble further to the Temple of Apollo where I would uncover the ornately carved corner of an altar my children and I had buried years earlier to hide it from those people who are compelled to scratch their names on unguarded antiquities. A second altar, which stood exposed, had lost a delicate bunch of grapes and a twirl of laurel to a passing vandal. The wound stood out in a clean gash against the weathered marble. After our wander in the ruins we would make our way back to the beach for a last swim before returning to the boat.

Once I had conducted a roll call the anchor would be raised and Captain Ahmet would take us to a tiny undis-covered beach on the mainland. Here while I instructed our party to spread towels over as large an area as possible, Bülent would light the portable barbecue and a lunch of Turkish meatballs with salad would be served, followed by great slabs of watermelon. The spreading of towels was to ensure that if any other boat did invade our beach there would be little room for the non-invited to settle comfortably. Once when a boat packed with beer-swilling sun wor-shippers tried to anchor, one of our party, the dean of an English cathedral, waded out to speak to them. We watched as the tourists on board made their captain under-stand that they didn't want to stop. Our Very Reverend swam back as they moved out to sea, and with a huge smile on his face he said, "I introduced myself and told them they were fortunate to have arrived in time to join our prayer meeting, due to start any minute." With a laugh he added that such a tactic always worked.

On one occasion as I finished my speech at the temple, a woman approached me and asked if I would mind telling her family a little about the island. They were a family from New York who were on a cruise around the Aegean but their guidebook didn't include Cedraea. My group raced off for their swim and I prepared to give the Americans a quick tour. With a painfully firm handshake the woman introduced herself as Erma Grubb and proceeded to introduce the Grubb family. As I gave my name, husband Grubb commented on how unusual my Christian name was. I refrained from making the obvious reply and proceeded to give them a potted history. As I finished I received another bone-crunching handshake, and as Erma profusely thanked me she said, "Your English is wonderful...it is almost as if it is your first language."

When Jane took over my job, she organised sheets for the guests to fill in listing the tours they wished to do, and by bullying Selim and myself made the whole of our little operation more efficient. One of the first things she decided was our need for a Turkish-bath tour. In typical Jane style she inspected the Marmaris and Muğla hamams and settling on the historic one in Muğla, she arranged with the manager for us to have the place closed to the public for a couple of hours every second Saturday afternoon. I was, she announced, to front up at the bath sometime the previous week to have a practice run. The whole idea of being half naked with a group of tourists in a room full of steam was dreadful and I neglected to go for my trial run, sort of hoping that by ignoring the existence of this new tour, it would simply go away.

Unfortunately, the hamam was not struck by lightning and Saturday afternoon found me pretending to a bus crammed to the seams that Turkish baths were old hat to me. Somehow I got through the whole ordeal and was quickly addicted to our bi-weekly trip.

One week we had a guest in the group who thought he was upper class; not only did he think he was, but he told everyone he was. Sitting on a marble slab with his hamam towel wrapped around his waist, he had neglected to keep his knees together. I was wondering if I should go across and mention it when a genteel old lady sitting with her sister signalled me to join them. Patting my hand she said, "Don't bother dear, we've never seen an upper-class pair before."

CHAPTER 14.

THAT SUMMER SEEMED to race; the children with their gang, old friends from Saudi Arabia and other guests had come and gone. In early autumn we were left with the memories of the minor disasters along with all the joys of meeting so many delightful people in the course of caring for the tourists. We vaguely talked of driving to Lebanon to visit Selim's sister and other family members before we embarked on the building of our real home in the following spring. Meanwhile we were happy to laze away the days before the onset of winter.

The architect who was to design us a traditional house knew exactly what we should have. He enthusiastically showed us plans which included a sunken marble pool complete with fountain, slap-bang in the middle of the salon. I had visions of having to peer round the water-jet to see guests on the other side of the room. The main bathroom had an oyster shell-shaped bath raised on a plinth. He proudly explained that pressure-adjustable water jets would shoot out of the sides of the bath. I found the thought quite frightening. Selim gently set him right, so we thought, but a week later he returned with new sketches which had given us a six-foot diameter chandelier as the focal point of the salon, and the bath had been replaced by a round Jacuzzi. This time our more forceful reactions prompted him to tell us that he was not only an architect but also an artist. He was to have full control of the design and the furnishings. In the quiet voice we family members recognise as deadly, my husband explained that our artist-cum-architect was not Christopher Wren; he was, in fact, a man who practised his trade in a backwater. He emphasised the point that we were building a house, not a palace. From then on the plans were more down to earth, apart from the bidet he slipped into the bathroom plans. The sketch had it positioned with one side flush with the wall; the acrobatics necessary to use it were mind-boggling, and it was immediately obvious that the man had never actually clapped eyes on one.

By January the plans were passed and the officious greenies had visited to ensure we were not cutting down too many of the Australian eucalyptus trees which they seemed to think were native to the area. Within a few weeks the land was covered with piles of lumber and mountains of cement bags, and a team of men with wheelbarrows were bringing loads of sand and gravel from the road. This time I kept out of the way and let Selim be the one to tear his hair out over the day-to-day problems.

The octagonal central salon with an 18-foot stud would have its own canopy, like an umbrella raised above the surrounding multi-angled roofs. The four longer walls of the eight-sided room had four square rooms off them and the four gaps between became six-sided lumps. It looked rather impractical, but this traditional use of space turned out to be extremely efficient. The lump I chose to pretentiously call the conservatory, positioned three yards from an inlet of the river, became our favourite area of the house.

By the second week of May it was finished and our first group of tourists for the season insisted on helping us move the thirty meters from the cottage. Nothing was packed and goods were passed hand to hand, while a group of women arranged things in the new rooms as they saw fit. Although it was by other people's standards a very small house, to us after the cottage it was huge. That evening the whole crew took us out to dinner, and back in our new home we climbed into our bed, made up by women who were paying for maid service in their holiday package.

One cold night when the house was not much more than a skeleton, we saw a flickering light coming from the inside. Selim went over to investigate and came back asking if we had any spare blankets. The light came from a fire lit by one of the workers. He was a seventeen-year-old orphan who had come south to seek his fortune. With nowhere to live, he had happily taken it upon himself to act as night watchman. His bedding consisted of one thin and well-worn blanket.

Next day one of our tents was erected further down the land and Coşkun furnished it with one of our camp beds and artistically-positioned apple boxes. Over the weeks he acquired a camp stove, a piece of carpet and a three-and-a-half legged table. On his day off he would busy himself with cleaning his home and would bake delicious cakes which he proudly shared with the workers and us.

Soon after we had settled in the new house, Selim commented that he thought Coşkun intended to make the tent a permanent home. He had gone down to visit and noted a cement floor had been laid and geraniums planted outside the flap. The boy considered us family and the tent was a real home, how could we tell him it was time to move on? Fortunately the problem was solved by the owner of the second tour company, who met our orphan while visiting the village. Seeing Coşkun's pride in his home, this kindly tour operator decided an odd-job man was needed, and here was just the person he was looking for.

A few months later Coşkun came racing in the gate, so excited he could hardly speak. Up in the village there was a mobile home for sale...a real house, he kept saying. If Selim would loan him the money to buy it, he would make weekly repayments. It was so ridiculously cheap that Pog and his friends went off to view the house. It was a gleaming 12-foot square tin shed. The group of young students were so touched that anyone could be so over the moon about a hut that when Pog called for donations the needed forty pounds sterling was raised within minutes. Selim borrowed a van and when the pieces were delivered everyone helped to lay a cement floor, and next day Coşkun's new home was erected. Saus went to Muğla and came back with a roll of carpet, curtains and a bedspread. I donated a tin of sage-green paint, which once applied to the exterior, made the walls almost invisible as they blended in with the eucalyptus leaves at the end of the garden.

That summer the government embarked on an ambitious road building plan all over Turkey. The villages in the hills suddenly had roads, and trucks arrived in Dereköy with huge machines which were installed at the back of the post office. Within weeks we all had real telephones. To be able to pick up a phone and contact not only the village but the world was a heady experience.

No longer did we have to go to the post office or leave the village to make phone calls, and the system London had set up to courier messages to us was no longer necessary.

Within weeks of the arrival of the telephones, a large box arrived on the flight with our tourists. Inside was a fax machine which the company wanted us to install so they could send us passenger lists. Neither of us had seen a fax machine at close quarters before and it took some time to hook it up. With Selim reading aloud each step of the process, I fed a message into the machine and jumped back as the paper began to move between the rollers. We were amazed when a second whirring noise produced a second piece of paper which stated, "Transmitting OK." Rather pleased with ourselves, we went off to make coffee, wondering how long it would be before the London office received our message.

We had hardly sat down with our drinks when the machine rang twice and started the whirring sound again. Standing over it we watched in amazement as paper began to chug out the "transmitting OK" slot. It went on and on; we thought sheets of paper would come out, but no, it was like a very wide toilet roll curling in piles on the floor. We wondered if something was amiss, but the pages were numbered so it couldn't be some fault in the wiring. Eventually it stopped and we had our first complete fax...all forty-seven pages of it.

Not long after the arrival of this amazing machine, Ekrem Bey telephoned from the post office to ask if he could send a British tourist down to us. This man was very distressed. He needed to use a fax machine and we had the only such gadget in the village. A very trendy-looking man arrived and explained that he was a director of a well-known English company, and there was a business crisis. For the next few days, he practically lived at our place, using the fax and our metered telephone. He was charming, grateful, and polite, but obviously thought we were such simpletons that what he was shouting into the phone and receiving at all hours on the fax would mean nothing to us. Often, when he had gone off for a few hours, a message would arrive, headed URGENT in huge type. By the third day, it was obvious that his company was the victim of a hostile bid from another prestigious UK company. So far it was all hush-hush, but it would hit the news soon, as his company looked as if it would have to admit defeat.

We know zilch about the business world, but when our visitor was not around we telephoned friends who do, and earned enough money on the stock market to upgrade our car. To this day I am not sure if we were guilty of insider trading.

Soon after his arrival Selim had begun the procedures to become a Turkish citizen. This involved a dozen trips to Istanbul, and at no stage did we know the next move. Nothing would be heard for months and then he would have to appear for an eye test. A few weeks later there would be a summons for an ear test. On several occasions after months had elapsed, our lawyer would chase things up and a summons would arrive for yet another test.

Two years later he was still not a Turkish citizen and when inquiries were made in Istanbul it appeared that his paperwork had disappeared without a trace. While the lawyer tried to follow up the problem through a maze of government departments, I grew more and more angry. I would go see the President. I would camp outside his official residence until he saw me. I would do this, I would do that. All intention, no action.

One afternoon soon after Coşkun's new house was installed at the end of the garden we decided to visit Marmaris. Selim went off to visit a friend living on his boat in the marina while I shopped. We had arranged to meet at a friend's carpet store and arriving at our meeting place, I noticed a fleet of sleek limousines parked nearby. On inquiring as to who was visiting the town I was told it was President Özal. He was at a restaurant four doors down. Without stopping to think logically I leapt into action.

Leaving my handbag and shopping with a much-bemused friend, I made for the restaurant. Pushing through the crowd I could see the President sitting eating ice-cream, surrounded by the members of the cabinet. When I crossed the invisible barrier between the guards and the public, a tall *jandarma* barred my way. When I told him I wished to speak to the President, he gave me a firm push back into the crowd and said what roughly translates as, "Push off, you stupid woman."

Far from deterred, I looked for another access. Approaching the rear of the restaurant from the back street, I climbed over a barricade of piled up tables and chairs. I slipped quickly through the kitchen and suddenly I was in the forecourt within yards of the President. Men moved slowly towards me with their hands tucked in their jackets, Napoleon style. A huge man was slouching at a table near the President; he said something and beckoned me over. In Turkish I tried to explain why I wanted to speak to the President. He had no English and my Turkish was feeble. While I stuttered the President, who was watching, gave a nod and the large man waved me towards him.

The President listened to my pathetic Turkish for a painful thirty seconds, and then asked in perfect English if I would prefer to speak in my own language. He listened patiently as I explained the problem, and asked a few questions before asking me to find my husband and bring him to the restaurant immediately.

Completely unfit, I started to run along the waterfront to the marina. That waterfront must be more than half a mile long but I made it, staggering towards our friend's yacht dragging air into my lungs like someone just saved from drowning. The boat was silent, nobody was there. At that moment a marina guard asked if he could help me, I gabbled something about my husband and the President as I still tried to get enough air. This young man must have instantly decided that I wasn't a nut case and took over the situation. Grabbing my arm, he bustled me out the back of the marina and barked directions to a taxi-driver. Every time we reached a roadblock he leapt out of the taxi waving his marina walkie-talkie and shouted to the police to remove the barricade. The police must have thought he was a secret service man. Both he and the taxi-driver were enjoying themselves thoroughly. As we went through the last roadblock onto the main road we stopped. Coming towards us was the President in an open topped limousine with a line of sleek black cars behind him.

Leaving the taxi, I stood in the road, and as the vehicle drew close the President called out, "Where is your husband?" When I replied that I couldn't find him I got a cheery wave and the assurance that he would solve the problem. I stood on the road verge in tears, my great chance bungled; I hadn't thought to write down Selim's name and one could not really expect the President to remember the details.

As I stood there one of the cars in the entourage suddenly swerved, nearly running over my toes. The back door opened and there lounging across the seat was the large man who had spoken to me initially. He who had previously no knowledge of the English language said in English, "Where is your husband?" Following my reply he leaned forward and shouted, "The President wishes to see your husband NOW. FIND him and bring him to the Turban Hotel immediately." With that, the car swung back onto the road and zoomed off to catch up with the open-topped limo ahead.

No way were my two helpers going to leave me, and all three of us made our way to where, by now, Selim should be waiting for me. Outside the carpet shop stood Selim surrounded by a crowd. When he had arrived a man had called out to him, "Quick, the President wants to see you, he is just getting into his car." Thinking it a joke, Selim had slowed his pace and replied that he didn't run after Presidents. The crowd was most impressed and it was only when he saw our friend holding my handbag that he realised something was going on. At that stage I arrived with my trusty aides. Selim was very cool as he said so very, very quietly, "What have you done?" I had no oppor-tunity to reply as my marina man once more took over and explained in rapid Turkish as the crowd pushed us towards the taxi. Once more roadblocks came down and we were soon in the hotel gardens. Mr. President was walking down a flight of steps to the beach; on seeing me he waved for me to join him. Holding onto my Turk's hand very firmly I moved to walk beside the President. Bodyguards closed in around us as I continued to clutch Selim's hand. As he started to ask once more where my husband was, he realised that my arm was disappearing between two of his minders' bodies and, not realising that he was ordering them to move apart, I gave a tug on Selim's hand. As the wall of bodies parted and I pulled, Selim came through the gap like a champagne cork.

We stopped walking and a long conversation ensued. Eventually the Minister for Internal Affairs was called to join us, and he asked that file numbers and details be written down and handed to him after the banquet.

"No," said the President. "Bring the details to me as soon as you have written them."

One week later our lawyer telephoned from Istanbul to announce that, due to all his hard work, Selim now had Turkish citizenship.

CHAPTER 15.

ONE MORNING MY Turk came back from the post-office looking as if he had been confronted by a ghost, and I suppose in some respects, he had.

After living in Paris for seven years following their exile from Turkey, Selim's grandparents with their four children had moved to Tripoli, Lebanon. There in the 1930's Selim's father had led the life of a young prince in an atmosphere akin to that of a Scott Fitzgerald novel. Life was a round of parties, riding, picnics, and evenings of dancing or games of cards. With not a care in the world at the age of twenty-two, he fell in love with a young woman from

Damascus. His mother did not approve but Prince Ibrahim could do no wrong, and after a whirlwind courtship they were married. Semiha the bride with four older brothers was the only daughter of a well placed family. Several years older than her husband, she was startlingly beautiful, spoiled and frivolous. The young couple continued the hedonistic life they both considered the norm. Unfortunately Semiha was soon pregnant and the lustre of love fast waned. By the time Selim was born the marriage was over and the couple had separated. Before the baby was a year old Semiha decided to hand the child over to Ibrahim's parents.

Princess Emine adored her first grandson and he was brought up in a home full of love. Ibrahim went overseas to work and would visit once a year. Laden down with extravagant gifts, he would entertain his son for a few days before disappearing again. Semiha was never mentioned in the house, and when Selim was sixteen he was told his mother was dead. In his thirties he was told by a close relative of his mother that she had remarried and had several more children before she died.

Now she had surfaced and was very much alive. A cousin of Ibrahim's living in Damascus had sent a newspaper clipping from a Syrian national paper. An elderly woman in an old people's home had been interviewed by a journalist and told of her marriage to a prince and of her son. He was her only child and she would not rest happy until she knew he was safe and well.

To me it was like a magic fairy tale; we must rush to Syria, find her, and an emotional reunion akin to those of the old black-and-white movies would ensue. Selim was less enthusiastic...at 56 years old it was difficult to learn one had a mother. He didn't know how to relate to the whole drama. His grandmother had always been his mother, and now suddenly there was this unknown person who, whether he liked it or not, was his mother. The article did not name where she was living and we had no idea what newspaper it had been cut from. The mystery deepened as we tried to fathom why the friend of her brothers had reported her death two decades earlier; and where were the siblings he had been told of? The only thing to do, we decided, was to go to Damascus and try to find her.

An Australian friend who was leaving on a 10-day tour of Syria and Petra in Jordan came to say goodbye and asked if there was anything I would like her to bring back from her trip. Half joking, I asked her to bring back the address of Selim's mother. Two weeks later, just days before our own departure, she was back with the names and addresses of the Damascus newspapers and the name of one old people's home.

We set off in early June to drive along the southern coast to Iskenderun and on to the Syrian border. The usually mild June temperatures suddenly soared, and we found ourselves slap-bang in the middle of a heat wave. Our old jalopy did not have the luxury of air-conditioning, and the dashboard was so hot the plastic started to smell. As dusk approached, we reached a large town and Selim instructed me to keep my eyes open for a family hotel. I didn't really care what kind of hotel it was, and when I saw a hotel sign I assured him it was a family hotel; he parked the car and I waited while he went in. Back almost immediately, he started the motor and turning to me quietly said, "When I ask for a family hotel it is for a reason. A very attractive woman was ready to show me a room until I mentioned my wife." Selim had spent the day driving over roads shimmering with heat, driving towards a mother he still wasn't sure he wanted to meet, and his stupid foreign wife had sent him to a brothel.

Next day we passed several crusader castles and villages with the houses built into the ruins of ancient settlements. We visited the church of St. Nicholas at Demre, the real home of the saint who inspired our modern Father

Christmas. That evening we arrived at a small border town where we planned to stay the night and leave early next morning for the border. It was the most miserable town I have ever encountered; the women were all closeted at home, or perhaps non-existent. The men were scruffy and surly; refusing to understand Selim's Istanbul Turkish, they turned their backs when he addressed them in Arabic. If you can conjure up the image of an Arab-flavoured Wild West town, this was it, even down to the knock-kneed horses. The staff of the one local eatery went out of their way to make us unwelcome, and we ate our *köfte sans* rice, *sans* salad from chipped plates, under the baleful watch of a group of ruffians playing cards. Fully dressed, I tried to sleep in a bed with less than dazzling white sheets while Selim dozed in a chair by the window, where he could keep an eye on the car. Early morning as we prepared to leave, we found one of my ancient thermos flasks was missing. Scratched and almost paintless, this flask had shared my adventures since I was lost in the Southern Alps of New Zealand as a teenager. The sullen night porter explained that the owner had taken it home with him to fill with hot tea for our journey. The fact that the owner must have unlocked our room and found the thermos at the bottom of my picnic basket was not mentioned. We would have to wait until the proprietor returned from an unexpected trip to Antakya, we were told. I just wanted to get out of the place, but Selim held firm: if my thermos was not found in ten minutes the police would be called. The porter took off at speed to the top floor of the hotel, and within minutes we were in the car with me clutching my tea-less flask.

The Turkish border was a collection of freshly painted buildings with strips of well-tended lawn and flowerbeds. The smartly dressed passport officers quickly processed our papers and we were driving through no-man's land to the Syrian border. As we passed rusting oil drums and the carcass of an abandoned car, Selim told me to put on my headscarf.

We stopped at a barred gate, and while one man watched us through the cracked window of a hut, a second wandered slowly to the car. Wearing camouflage fatigues, a Donald Duck tee-shirt and carrying an impressively large gun, he leaned in the driver's window and asked if we had any cigarettes. Selim fished under his seat and found a packet of Marlboro cigarettes, which he handed to the guard. The man wanted more, but was told that was all we had. In slow motion he moved to the barricade, lifted it and, spitting on the ground, he made his way back to the shade of the hut. We drove to the largest of the dilapidated buildings ahead and as we parked, a motley group of men jockeyed for position beside the driver's door. Negotiating with them, Selim chose one of them to ease our way through the formalities and I was left alone in the car. Every patch of shade harboured a badly dressed, gun-toting soldier. In the shade of a large veranda a group of men in jeans, unbuttoned shirts, triple-soled trainers and chunky gold medallions stood and eyed the car. With the car baking in the sun, time seemed to have stopped and I felt I had been under their watchful gaze for hours. As Selim returned, one of the watchers flicked his cigarette into the dust and made his way to my window. He put his hand on my arm and said in English, "My wife wants a leather jacket." Selim appeared to go into a demented frenzy, screaming in Arabic that I was a devout Muslim and how dare anyone molest me. Others joined the fray and Selim got more religious and frenzied by the minute. Eventually calm was restored, hands were shaken and all were brothers. We drove to the exit barricade, where Selim passed over another packet of Marlboro from under the seat and we were off into Syria.

"Those bastards were secret service," he said. I don't know which shocked me more, the incident or Selim swearing. Once away from the border, I started to laugh as it was explained to me that the request for a leather jacket would have pre-empted a search of the car, when anything the denim-clad gentlemen fancied would have disappeared. As to the Marlboro cigarettes, I was told one never travelled these routes without a supply. The trick was to know who the one-packet men were and who needed a more generous supply to oil the wheels of bureaucracy. The Suez Canal is a two-carton route, I was informed.

We drove along a good tar-sealed road; the few other cars we saw were old and, like the buses, were Russian. Almost without exception the vehicles had a poster of President Assad in the rear window. Walls and buildings sported the same picture, and occasionally we would pass a hoarding with the presidential family smiling down on us from a great height. The houses were raw cement with none of the olive-oil-tin planters full of geraniums so common on the Turkish side of the border. For lunch we stopped at a huge roadside restaurant, and it was here we saw for the first time the warmth of Syrian hospitality. A huge plate of hummus, the best I have ever tasted, tabbouleh, a mountain of mint and crisp lettuce with radishes so hot and crunchy they brought tears to the eyes, followed by plate after plate of köfte, kebab, mixed grills and beyti. Welcoming smiles surrounded us as we tried to do justice to a plate of fresh fruit. The bill came to less than five American dollars, and as we made our way to the car a waiter chased us to give us the bottle of water and packet of tissues which had come with the meal. Syria was not so bad after all, and my earlier apprehension was dissolving.

We arrived in Damascus just before dark, where we found the last room with a fan in the Sultan Hotel, opposite the Hijaz railway station. We dined by candlelight that evening in a rather posh restaurant where they mistook Selim for a famous Levantine; when he tried to put them right, the proprietor winked and said, "Of course, Monsieur, of course. Our lips are sealed." After such an adventurous trip we became a little tipsy on our glasses of mineral water as we were treated as VIPs who wished to remain anonymous. Next morning we ate in the small dining niche of the hotel and gazed at the handful of foreign tourists around us. Selim had discreetly passed the gnome-like waiter a pre-breakfast tip, which ensured piping hot toast and two extra dollops of butter.

As it was Sunday, Selim had planned a quiet day before we started our search on Monday. As he went down to check that the car still had four wheels and other basic necessities, I went to the reception desk with the phone number our friend Pam had given me. I asked the reception-ist to telephone the number and enquire if there was a resident named Semiha Ramadan. He looked very respect-ful and asked if we knew the Ramadans; when I said they were family, I had the feeling we had once again hit VIP mode. The conversation was long and I couldn't follow the rapid Arabic, when the man suddenly spoke to me. "Did you want to visit her?" he said. When I asked if she was there, he said that he was speaking to her. I stood shaking as he wrote down the address. When he said that she was concerned because she did not speak English, I told him to tell her I would take an interpreter with me. As he hung up Selim came out the elevator doors, and in a babbling rush of words I told him of the conversation and that she was expecting us immediately.

We drove through a suburb of tree-lined avenues where large villas hid behind high walls. We stopped at what looked like a five-star hotel, and in a gleaming foyer Selim asked for Semiha's room number. On the second floor we stood outside on open door with the number 27 in Arabic script. As Selim gazed at the numbers I looked into the room, and seated at the far end was a female version of Selim...dye the white hair and give her a cigar, and it was him.

At no stage in our plans had we been able to work out, if indeed we did find his mother, just how to break the news. One could hardly leap into the room of a frail and very ancient woman screaming, "Surprise!" This interpreter thing would, with luck, ease us in gently.

After my hesitant Arabic greetings, the dignified old lady inclined her head towards Selim.

"Who are you?" she asked.

"May I ask you some questions?" Selim said. When with a regal nod of her head she indicated yes, he said, "Do you remember Princess Emine?"

"Of course; she was my mother-in-law."

"Do you remember Ali Kenan?"

"Damat Ali Kenan," she said sharply, with a look of reproof at this upstart who neglected to use titles.

"Do you remember Prince İbrahim?"

With a small soft smile she said, "He was my husband."

"He was my father," Selim said in a quiet voice.

She sat silent and still. I could hear the clatter of the tea trolley in the hall. Tears were running down my face as she sat unmoving. After a minute or so, she turned her head and giving Selim an almost coquette-like smile, whispered, "Then you are my son." It was a statement, not a question, and as he nodded she looked up at him and holding out her hands she said, "Then I think you should kiss me."

As I sobbed all over the place and Selim started to explain how we had found her, the manageress of the home came into the room. She had been told that an English visitor had arrived, and had come to check. She stopped and took in the scene. Semiha was holding a strange man's hand and her other hand was stroking a distraught foreign woman. Semiha looked at her for a few seconds and then said, "Oh! Mrs. Habib, I don't believe you have met my son." At this Mrs. Habib shrieked, and the room filled with people. Mother and I giggled at her cool sense of humour, while Selim was hugged by a horde of women. I went out into the corridor to try to pull myself together, and watched as an elderly man with a walking frame raced at two miles an hour to each door, spreading the news. An old lady in a beautiful silk dress whizzed past me in a wheel chair to take the lift to the lower floor to pass on the news.

We made our excuses as the lunch trolley arrived, and promised to return in the late afternoon. Back at the hotel we shared our fears, which until now had been unspoken. Selim had been worried that we would find a mother who wanted to come and live with us, but Semiha had already told him she was very happy where she was. I confessed to the worry that we would find a dyed and painted geriatric socialite who would want to pull us into the whole middle-eastern family thing.

When we returned late afternoon, Selim's new family were there to meet him. A delightful cousin whose father-in-law was one of the most powerful men in Syria had left her bevy of bodyguards in the corridor; she treated them like a group of naughty children and it was easy to see they adored her. A male cousin who was thrilled to meet Selim was also a little stunned, as he hadn't known Semiha had ever had a child until earlier in the afternoon. Another older cousin was hell-bent on proving Selim was an impostor, but one look at mother and son silenced him. This man's father was the one who had, years ago, sent the message of Semiha's death, and it was now obvious that family monies had been the motive. But the culprit was dead so we let the matter lie.

Next day mother and son sat quietly and talked of the past. She told him her version of her life with Ibrahim and why she had not kept her child. It was a dramatic story, which I am sure she believed, but fact was hard to find in her tale. She had so thoroughly embroidered her memories of those times that it was kinder to just nod and listen. She had been a vain, spoiled young woman with no room for a child in her life; it was far more pleasant in old age to believe he had been ripped from her arms.

On our fourth morning Selim received a phone call from the friend who was looking after our tourists at home in Dereköy. Her father had been rushed to hospital and we would have to cut our stay short and head for home. We said our goodbyes and, armed with a letter for the border guards, we headed home. What our powerful new relative had written we do not know, but when we handed it to the first slouching soldier he quickly buttoned up his tunic, saluted and rushed into his ramshackle booth to make a phone call. As he raised the gate, a jeep followed by a cloud of dust came to meet us and a portly officer effusively welcomed us to his border post. The leather-jacketed thugs of less than a week before were now charming young men who guarded the car while we had tea in the commander's office. Our passports were whisked away and returned stamped in minutes, with no mention of the usual less-than-legitimate fees.

Soon home on Turkish soil, Selim asked if there was any town on the way I would like to explore. When I pointed out we should hurry, I learned that there had been no phone call from Dereköy. While he had enjoyed meeting his mother and relatives, he had had enough. He wanted the quiet of home to think it all out.

CHAPTER 16.

WHILE OUR COMMUNITY was designated a village, we received limited finances from the powers beyond the mountains. This had been no problem, as there was nothing we really needed. As tourism started to develop in the village, we found there was a multitude of things we couldn't live without. Street lights, paved roads, public lavatories and so on suddenly became vital.

We had to become a township to get a larger share of the public purse. To do this, we needed to have a permanent population of more than 2000, a number way beyond our realm even with our enthusiastic breeding record. The village elders came up with the answer: we all had to invite everyone possible to stay in our houses during the weekend of the census. Dolmuş-loads of relatives and friends arrived, lured by the promise of a riotous weekend. All we required of the visitors was that they be permanent residents on the census forms. Fortunately, we had my sister and her husband - retired missionaries - staying with us. We didn't burden them with the dishonesty of it all, but with their signatures we had done our bit for the village.

Other houses bulged and several family feuds were rekindled in the tedious hours all were forced to wait in the confines of their homes. The three sisters of Teoman Bey have not spoken to each other since.

The tension was palpable in the *muhtar's* office as an unofficial count of the forms was done and much back-slapping ensued when the final count was 2,070.

Within weeks we'd become very important and politicians added us to their campaign itineraries. The first to arrive was the Bee Party (actually the Motherland Party...their symbol is a honeycomb with bees) and the town was festooned with the appropriate flags and banners. A nice young man with hesitant speech spoke from the top of a bus and we cheered every statement. It started to rain but we all stayed and clapped as a petulant child presented the speaker with flowers. The next day we were all out in the rain again, new flags and bunting had replaced the bees, and this time we wore little lapel stick-pins in the shape of a horse on our raincoat collars. We all cheered the pretty lady who spoke, and our sulky child, now with a cold, re-enacted the flower ceremony.

As more parties visited, we continued to play our role as hosts. We were most impressed by the parties with fancy buses and put on a good show for all but one. Continuing inclement weather had forced a change in the location, and as a fleet of sleek black cars parked outside the teahouse, one reversed over our town drunk, then the driver shouted at him!

Now, we have only one town drunk and he is a scholar and a poet. Whether his poetry is any good I don't know, but the locals have great respect for his stanzas. Other towns can muster up a bevy of sots, but we have one - a very good one - and we are fond of him. The *muhtar* took Cem İki to hospital and we all turned our back on this lot, who hadn't even got a bus. We made our ways home or back to work. This business of entertaining all these outsiders was getting a bit too much. Most of us were going to vote for Fat Ali's brother in any case: as the sole candidate born and raised in the village, he was our only choice, really.

Nobody in Dereköy was usually very bothered about the national elections, but this time as they and the local elections drew nearer, the town was abuzz with political rhetoric. We don't go in for sound bites here, it's more of a sound chunk which prevails. One of the perks of country life is that one's vote in local elections is very important; it really could be the deciding factor.

Cars covered with flags cruised the town with loud-speakers playing the parties' jingles. Vacant shops were turned into party headquarters, where dark-suited men huddled at all hours. We were presented with nice little brochures which promised the earth, and there was bunting everywhere.

We had to be careful to ensure the right pamphlet was on the coffee table when party officials dropped in to admire Selim's boat. As these concerned and friendly citizens never appeared at any other time, I was tempted to be a little terse, but Selim was rather imperious and insisted on my being gracious. This I was, and he was pleased that I behaved myself. In fact, I went the whole hog and took malicious pleasure in watching them juggle the dainty little cups filled with lapsang souchong, the sliced lemon, the cake plates, cake forks, damask napkins and sugar tongs. A few families actually announced who they were going to vote for, which was foolhardy to say the least. If their man lost, they'd get four years of potholes in the road outside their house or shop.

Our old mayor was hoping to serve another term. He had done a terrific amount for the town. There was the children's park, with its fibreglass elephant slide and beer kiosk. The new football pitch was beautiful, and if we ever get a football team, it's ready and waiting. The huge expanse of pink concrete with the fountain and statue was perhaps not his greatest success, but one has to admit, it demonstrates progress. Fortunately most have forgotten the water-pipe fiasco, when those with lesser clout had no water for two months. He suddenly realised the value of the conservation society, which was amazing seeing he had tried to wipe out the otter colony the year before.

The second candidate was a smaller, dapper man who has made a lot of money. He, like the incumbent, sports the obligatory chain and bracelet but, being of a less imposing stature, he looked more like a bookie's tout than a Turkish small-town politician. This chap took over his father's restaurant years ago and hit on a novel gimmick. He actually put tablecloths on the tables and, as if this wasn't revolutionary enough, he kept replacing them with clean ones. This one act has made his fortune. The restaurant serves food that is a travesty of Turkish cuisine, with farmed trout that taste of farm. His enemies allude to shady land deals, but I believe the money was simply generated by a generous supply of tablecloths.

A week after our old mayor was re-elected the town was still gripped by the results. The restaurateur was very dignified about losing, but some of his followers hinted at foul play in the counting of the votes. There was talk of an enquiry.

Özcan the hairdresser was so emotional and angry about some aspect of the whole election saga that, as he shouted his views at me, he nearly pulled my hair out by the roots. When I staggered out of his shop to meet Selim, he looked at me and said, "I thought you were going to have your hair done."

A few days after the results were announced we had a water cut which lasted all night. Next morning we got the news hot from the postmaster. The man in charge of the town's water supply had openly campaigned for the wrong man and had been given his marching orders the day after the elections. It appears that the various waterpipe junctions are turned on and off with a key. As he left his office, along with his name plate he took the pipe junction keys. After three days of nurturing his anger, he turned off the water supply and threw away the keys. Who reconnected our water and how, I have never found out.

Early that autumn, as part of our preparation for the coming winter, we decided to have the roof cleaned. A small, gnarled and ancient gnome spent days up there, removing leaves, broken tiles and branches jettisoned by the eucalyptus trees. As a roof-cleaning expert, he would not deign to clean the piles of debris mounting up at ground level, so we spent a week carting away all that he had tossed down.

When the hard driving rains arrived, we had leaks in every room - not gentle drips but vigorous torrents. One room had so many streams of water pouring from the ceiling that the floor was wall to wall buckets, basins and large saucepans, which had to be emptied almost hourly. It came as no surprise that our roofing specialist was nowhere to be found. The problem was overcome by swathes of plastic held down by bricks, which gave the outside of the house a quality that Christo would have applauded.

Soon winter was on its way. The terrapins, always the first to hibernate, had disappeared. The little grebe, moorhens and water rail which winter in our pond were back from their summer travels. As the frankincense trees shed their leaves and the wild cyclamen begin to flower, our thoughts returned to our leaky roof. A roofer with a sheaf of bona-fide references was hired to sort it out. Every tile had to be removed and a liner laid before they were replaced. All this was to cost the equivalent of a winter-long stay in a five-star hotel, but I cheered up when he promised his helper would clean everything at ground level.

Spare tiles and rolls of black, linoleum-like liner were

purchased and the work began. The helper was the worker one dreams of, but never really believes exists. This man cleaned every last twig, leaf and lump of broken tile. Not once did he slink off for a cigarette or ponder the world while leaning immobile on his broom. Assured that my supervision was not needed, I decided to tackle a large area of the garden that had been neglected throughout the unusually long and hot summer. For four days I laboured, pruning, weeding and splitting up overgrown clumps of plants. On the fifth morning, with only an hour or so to put in to complete the transformation, I was walking towards the garden when I suddenly stopped. Something had totally destroyed the whole area. There were huge holes, with tree roots pointing skyward. Nothing short of a herd of elephants could have caused such havoc.

People who know me may find it hard to believe, but I was speechless. Rushing back to the house, making babbling noises and waving my arms, I dragged my bemused husband from his breakfast to survey the scene. "Pig," he said. "Wild boar." At that moment Yılmaz the roofer arrived. "Pig," he said.

Across the river, wild boar live in the conservation area; we hear them crashing in the reeds at full moon. But not once since those first weeks in the cottage have any crossed the river. The problem was immediately compounded. We live within the boundaries of the conservation reserve, which means we can take pot-shots at a human entering our garden for nefarious purposes under the cover of dark. But a pig, no! There had been a nasty hunting accident only days before, so the *jandarma* chief would not turn a blind eye, or even a deaf ear to gunshots in the night.

Selim went off to ask the *jandarmas* for advice while Mr. Wonder Helper and I started repairing the damage, a labour that took us the whole day. Selim returned with the gloomy news that his gun would be confiscated if he were to shoot in a protected area. So, in the afternoon he built a long "pig-frightening fence". This, the locals assured us, would deter any pig. Gazing at the tin cans and strips of plastic dangling from pig-height string, I wondered how long I'd have to live with this unsightly addition to the garden.

That evening we had a dinner engagement but managed to excuse ourselves to be home in time to frighten the pig, should it reappear. On our gate was a note from our neighbours. Sorry, it said, but they had come home at 10.30, and the pig had already come and gone. Trust us to get the one boar that didn't know that it should come after midnight - as well as not being the slightest bit fazed by our magnificent barricade. Fortunately the damage was minimal this time; perhaps our neighbours' return had scared it off. Nevertheless, with the garden ruined and piles of roofing material stacked everywhere along with the rubble from the roof, our paradise looked anything but.

Next day Selim spent a lot of time rummaging in the attic and stayed in his workshop for hours while I, once again, put the garden to rights. That evening he had an appointment to see the big number-one *jandarma*, who had promised help in finding a solution. Selim had hardly driven up the drive when I heard the pig moving in the reeds on the edge of the garden. Judging by the noise, it had to be enormous. I telephoned for Selim to come home and five minutes later he arrived with two sergeants with pistols and a young recruit with a machine pistol. The two NCOs were nonchalant about the whole thing, but the young conscript, a country boy with hunting savvy, had a different attitude. He prefaced his pig-hunting instructions to his seniors with the words, "Respected Sirs," then explained graphically how dangerous a cornered or wounded wild boar could be. After eyeing their puny handguns, the two decided to allow the private to form the vanguard of the assault, while they provided support from the rear. These intrepid lads rushed to the reeds, where the noise and movement suddenly stopped. They reassured us the pig had fled across the river and would trouble us no more. Should it return at any time in the future they would come back to ambush it. They were thanked profusely - without us mentioning that if the pig had crossed the river, it had done so with no sound of a splash.

After they had gone, Selim explained his plan; he had got his hunting bow and arrows down from the attic and was going to shoot the boar. The law talked about guns; nobody had mentioned any other type of weapon. The poor darling - it was more than forty years since he had hunted outside Ankara with a bow and arrow, but I certainly wasn't about to tell him he was past it.

Most of the arrows had lost their feathers to the moths, but two were intact and he had found two razor sharp hunting tips. The bow, bought in America twenty-five years ago, he had never used.

We opened the double doors from the conservatory and Selim positioned two chairs inside, while I laid bait thirty meters away. I was rather sad to see such a special person deluding himself in this way, but at least nobody would hear when he missed. When it was all over I'd make him a nice cup of cocoa and talk of something else. Meanwhile, I decided to play along with the charade.

We sat in silence in the conservatory with a clear view of the damp bread and potato peelings - manna from heaven to a pig, I'm told. On a low table in front of us sat the bow which Selim would occasionally lift up and hold in what I imagined was a hunting position. Sitting still and watching a pile of food scraps in the moonlight didn't turn out to be the most enthralling of after-dinner entertainments, and I was soon itchy, achy and very bored. After hours and hours (in reality it was only 10 o'clock), moving towards the bow my archer whispered, "It's coming." But just at that moment a speedboat roared up the river, causing our pig to retreat to the undergrowth. Twenty minutes later it was once again coming close when our neighbours dropped what sounded like a crate of bottles and we were back to square one again.

At eleven o'clock, while I was trying to work out how to break it gently that this was a rather pathetic farce, Selim stood up and tried out the bow again. But this time there was a twang...then a sound of rushing like a whirlwind followed by very loud grunts, then silence. I hadn't even seen the pig. Our neighbours Hans and Günter came rushing to the fence, wondering why they hadn't heard a shot and offering to come and take the body away. Selim said that to be safe we must leave it for half an hour, then we could look in the reeds. I was so proud of him I thought I'd explode, but he seemed to think it was all very normal.

After we'd had a cup of coffee and stretched our aching muscles, the neighbours joined us to hunt in the bamboo and the undergrowth on the fringes of the river. Hans and Günter, eager to relieve us of the carcass, arrived with a fishing spear-gun and a pitchfork, but there was no need for caution. There was our pig - not the envisaged giant, but a yearling - shot close to the heart.

Selim was the hero of the district and Mehmet the grocer pointed out to all his customers that Selim's ancestors were famed as archers. Although we are both anti-hunting and keen conservationists, we feel no guilt over our adventure. Our wonder worker, who chooses who he will or will not work for, was so impressed next day that he has offered to come any time we ask.

CHAPTER 17

BY 1986 WHEN the cottage was finished I had settled into my new life in Turkey. My Turkey was different from the Turkey of the big cities and towns. There was no village water pipe to the 'backblocks' where my home was hidden by the trees, so I pumped water from the river to a tank balanced on a high platform made of stout eucalyptus branches. The village often had power cuts lasting four or five days, which found me carrying buckets from the river and cooking by candle light. I carried my drinking water from the village and hired the local taxi when I needed a new gas bottle for the oven, manhandling the bottle the last 200 yards down the track. My washing machine was the same brand of large plastic bowl as the other village women used. My little radio worked on batteries and apart from lighting and the water pump I had no other need for electricity.

The villages in the mountains had no roads or amenities and the villagers would come down the narrow goat tracks on foot when they needed to shop or visit the doctor in the village two or three miles kilometres further along the main road.

I used to walk to the road by balancing on the stepping stones crossing the little stream, then make my way up the track to the gravel road which led to the village centre. The road, wide enough for a tractor, was flanked by hedgerow filled with birds and wildlife. One could sometimes hear a vehicle in the distance but usually there were only the age-old sounds of nature. I would pass Baba's tiny ramshackle house and his citrus orchard, and a few fields further along were the homes of two sisters. One house was large and imposing with metal doors and window frames set off with awesome cement columns, while the other was small and poor. At the sisters' land one turned right to follow the road meandering through a grove of pines to the village centre.

This walk could be completed in fifteen minutes but would often take hours; sometimes I would be waylaid at one of the three houses on route, stopping for a chat or a tea. The sisters who had not spoken to each other for twenty years would vie with each other to lure me onto their own patch to snub the enemy over the fence. On other days I would meet the camel man, or a tractor would pass, slowing to a crawl to avoid covering me with dust. Often the driver would stop and I would balance myself side-saddle on the huge mudguard and ride in style to the post office. More often than not, I would meet no one but stop to watch the birds. One evening I spent an hour watching a porcupine, another afternoon I saw my first slowworm. At dusk there would be the occasional fox and just once, I glimpsed a pine marten as it shot across the road in front of me. The hedgerow was full of flowers in the spring, and later a mass of berries of varying hues.

The beach bordered by marshland was perhaps a little scruffy, as was the pier where the fishing boats bobbed in a long line. Several very village-y restaurants and half a dozen houses were the only buildings in the area.

In the late 1980's the village water pipes were renewed and extended so potable water no longer had to be manhandled from the water fountain near Mehmet's grocery shop. Massive pylons straddle the mountains to bring a regular supply of electricity to us all. My stepping stones have been replaced with a stout bridge and a gravelled lane comes to our gate. The tractor-wide road to the village is now two-laned tarmac, with speed bumps. The hedgerows have gone and the road is bordered by concrete walls and municipal garbage bins, behind which stand rows of villas. The lemon, orange and mandarin trees have been replaced by palms and bougainvillaea. The birds and wildlife have decamped and the sounds of sleek cars whizzing along the tarmac, of radios and yappy pet dogs fill the air. Sometimes in the early evening we hear the otters calling, but they are rarely seen these days, driven into the backwaters by the river traffic. The lower slopes of the mountainside are covered with houses with solar panels on the roofs glinting in the sun, and satellite dishes adorn the balconies. Tractors are rarely seen and the camel man has gone...I don't know where. The newcomers sit on their tiled patios and enjoy country life as they cook dinner on gas barbecues. The sisters are rarely seen loitering in their gardens, as they are too busy running their houses as bed and breakfast pensions.

The beach is now swept daily, with a proud row of palm trees cutting through the jumble of plastic sun-lounges and bright umbrellas. The pier with a new row of palms has been paved, and fishing boats jostle for the few moorings left after the large disco-tour boats have returned at the end of the day. The marsh abutting the beach has been drained and a hotel now occupies this acreage: a hotel where foreign tourists can imbibe the way of life in a small Turkish town without having to eat Turkish food or meet any Turk other than their English-speaking waiter.

I rarely walk to the village now, but if I do, I am in danger of being squished by a passing car. My kitchen is a wonder of modern science with deepfreeze and microwave while water (minus the river weed) gushes from the tap. Three phone lines are an absolute necessity for the telephone, fax and e-mail. Along with the other washerwomen of the village, a fully automatic machine has updated my plastic bowl. Our one decrepit village taxi has been superseded by a fleet of gleaming vehicles, not that I would need one as my gas bottle is delivered to the door. The quaint little shepherdess who spins as she guards her flock is still to be seen on the outskirts of the town; what she thinks of the tourists who photograph her would be interesting to know.

Baba Macit's mandarin and orange trees have gone, replaced by beautiful villas. Baba sits morosely on the porch of his magnificent new home and pines for his trees. Ekrem Bey at the post office never really got over the arrival of automatic telephones, and is pathetically pleased if anyone wanders into the post office to post a letter.

Behind the old port is a rubbish dump spreading across acres of what was once pristine forest. Swimming pools, neglected once the summer people head for home, are a haven for mosquito larvae. Many foreigners have chosen to make Dereköy their home and apart from one man from Sri Lanka, none of them have made an effort to be part of the community.

All the new buildings are built in the Ula-Muğla style and the building laws forbid anything higher than two floors. Land is worth a fortune, as more and more people want to sit behind their walls and enjoy what they imagine is country life. With modernisation things may have become easier but we've lost the essence of country living. Newcomers to the town all comment on the beautiful setting and the lovely houses. Yes, it is beautiful, but it no longer has character. Dereköy has become a soulless summer town.

Last week they cut down the mulberry tree and demolished the teahouse to make way for yet another block of shops.

The time has come for us, like the camel man, to move on....

GLOSSARY

Abaya: The all-enveloping robe worn in the Middle East

Baba: Father

Bayram: Religious holiday

Beyti: Middle Eastern meat dish

Boncuk: Bead, a good-luck talisman

Dolmuş: From the word dolma, meaning stuffed, as in stuffed vine leaves. A dolmuş is a mini-bus, which true to its name is usually stuffed to bursting point.

Hamam: Turkish bath house

Hummus: A Middle Eastern dip made with chickpeas and sesame paste

İmam: An Islamic priest

İmam Bayıldı: A Turkish dish, translated it means 'the İmam fainted.' Folklore says it was given this name when the İmam fainted with delight after tasting it. Another version claims that the İmam fainted when he learned how much expensive olive oil his wife had used in preparing the dish.

Jandarma: Gendarme

Kebab: Middle Eastern meat dish

Köfte: Middle Eastern meat dish

Muhtar: Village headman

Muska: Amulet

Pompa: Pump

Simit: A crunchy bread ring

Tabbouleh: Middle Eastern salad.

Tavla: Backgammon

Vali: Governor of a province